RE-IMAGINING CHILD PROTECTION

Towards humane social work with families

Brid Featherstone, Sue White and Kate Morris

MT

First published in Great Britain in 2014 by

Policy Press
University of Bristol
6th Floor
Howard House
Queen's Avenue
Clifton
Bristol BS8 1SD
UK
t: +44 (0)117 331 5020
f: +44 (0)117 331 5367
pp-info@bristol.ac.uk
www.policypress.co.uk

North America office:
Policy Press
c/o The University of Chicago Press
1427 East 60th Street
Chicago, IL 60637, USA
t: +1 773 702 7700
f: +1 773 702 9756
sales@press.uchicago.edu
www.press.uchicago.edu

British Library Cataloguing in Publication Data
A catalogue record for this book is available from the British Library

Library of Congress Cataloging-in-Publication Data
A catalog record for this book has been requested

ISBN 978 1 44730 801 0 paperback
ISBN 978 1 44730 802 7 hardcover

FSC
www.fsc.org
MIX
Paper from
responsible sources
FSC® C004309

Cover design by Andrew Corbett
Front cover: iStock
Printed and bound in Great Britain by CMP, Poole

2/10/15

Contents

Acknowledgements

The authors would like to thank all those who have contributed to the development of the ideas explored in this book. While its final production is our responsibility, we have appreciated the opportunities to debate and discuss our thinking with many valued friends and colleagues. We would also like to thank our families, who have offered us support and, most importantly, the time to write this book.

ONE

Introduction

> One of the important ways in which the meanings of children's lives may be constructed and become powerful is through the assumptions underpinning professional discourses, but such frameworks may reshape and arguably empty out the moral and political aspects of experience and suffering. (Ribbens McCarthy, 2013: 331)

Social workers are charged with entering the lives and moral worlds of families, many of whom have routinely experienced disrespect, and have longstanding histories of material and emotional deprivation. In entering such lives, social workers share with those they encounter universal experiences of loss and disappointment. However, there are additional issues that arise in the course of doing such a job involving the making of decisions that bring pain and hurt as well as joy and support with consequences that can endure for generations. This dual mandate (often known as care and control) is one to be treated with humility and seriousness.

Entering the homes and lives of those who routinely experience disrespect is a privilege but it is not a job for the fainthearted, especially in societies that are increasingly riven by hostility towards those who are vulnerable and in need. As the research evidence suggests, service users often feel fearful and powerless in their interactions with social workers, and this feeds into encounters that may be characterised by misunderstandings at best, and aggression at worst (Featherstone and Fraser, 2012a).

Increasingly, the work takes place in a very defensive climate and that defensiveness takes on particular forms from differing vantage points. Social workers have, for many decades, felt caught between a rock and a hard place, damned if they don't remove children and damned if they do. Their mandate is subject to fickle pendulum swings, with the terms usually set by others, from the government of the day to the media. It is perhaps not that surprising, therefore, that their self-perceptions are subject to the same volatile swings. In less frightening times, social workers seem more able to appreciate their power and service users' relative powerlessness, whereas in very defensive periods, the focus seems to shift to social workers seeing themselves as powerless. Indeed, the narrative of victimisation has become a very powerful one, and unfortunately can obviate the need for the most rigorous interrogation of work that is so consequential. It can also preclude ownership by social workers of the substantial powers they possess.

Academics can be perceived by social workers as either persecutory or out of touch with reality in a risk dominated audit society. In such a context, it is understandable that the profession may shrink from critique, or for academics to feel their role is to make visible or celebrate the good work that is done. We do not shrink from critique in this book as we consider the consequences are too grave for workers, families and the wider society if we continue to pursue the child protection task as it is currently. However, we do want to emphasise that this book has been written in a spirit of solidarity with all those who undertake the task and those who teach and research in this area. We want to deepen and extend the dialogue and debate in which we are currently engaged with practice communities and policy makers.

We have written this book for many reasons, but a key impulse has emerged in the course of our engagement with managers, practitioners and students through research, speaking at conferences or tutoring. More and more often we encounter some disquiet about contemporary policy and practice, and, in particular, anxiety that the social justice aspect of social work is being lost in a child protection project that is characterised by a muscular authoritarianism towards multiply-deprived families.

However, we are also motivated by the concern we feel when we hear the phrase "I'm only here for the child." We understand that the phrase supports the performance of a moral identity in a confusing and frightening landscape where there are multiple vulnerabilities and risks. However, for all its rhetorical and moral potency, it reflects, in our view, misrecognition of children's relational identities and we will argue that it is problematic ethically and practically.

We have also been influenced by our own research, and that of others, on service users' perspectives. As Melton (2009) has argued, too often the current system objectifies the children whom it seeks to protect and the parents it 'accuses'. Our research with parents suggests they are intimidated by child protection processes and feel fearful and powerless in their interactions with workers (Featherstone et al, 2011). Moreover, our research on system design supports the recognition from a range of international commentators of the 'systemic failure' of the child protection systems that have developed in 'Anglophone' countries. Lonne et al (2009) use the term 'Anglophone' to refer to the following:

US, Canada, UK, Australia and New Zealand. Although our specific focus is England, where we have been involved in practising, educating and researching for nearly three decades, it is abundantly clear that our concerns are shared more widely. Across countries, complex processes have developed that seem designed primarily to manage institutional risk (White et al, 2010) rather than to enable families to flourish within strong and supportive networks. We agree with those who argue that these processes are too costly, both economically and in human terms for all the stakeholders involved (Lonne et al, 2009).

In England, while there are particular elements of the policy and practice climate that are of profound concern to us at the time of writing this book, we suggest that these are just sharper manifestations of a more longstanding and problematic project. Our purpose is to interrogate this project but also to question and open up new possibilities and conversations.

Before introducing such possibilities and conversations, we need to do some preliminary ground clearing and state clearly what we are *not* arguing in this book. We are *not* arguing that adults, including parents and other adult family members, do not harm children deliberately or by acts of omission. We are *not* arguing that parents are never resistant or hostile to social workers. We are *not* arguing that the task of protecting children from such harms is not an absolutely essential and very valuable one: of course it is and must remain so. Our focus on social workers does not mean that we do not consider the role of other professionals or inter-professional working of vital importance. Of course we do, but in this book we are speaking to our own profession in order to ask questions about our ethics and practices.

We want to consider whether the frameworks used and underpinning assumptions in the child protection task, as it is currently constituted, are hollowing out important moral and political issues (Ribbens McCarthy, 2013) in their neglect of questions such as the following:

- Why do we use the language of the *child* and of child protection?
- What is lost and gained by such a language?
- Why is the language of family and family support so marginalised?
- Who is being protected, and from what, in a risk society?
- Given that the focus is overwhelmingly on those families who are multiply deprived, do services reinforce or ameliorate such deprivations?
- Is it ethically desirable to focus on rescuing children and leaving their parents behind in a society riven by inequalities?

- Why don't we explore and engage with mothers and fathers as subjects in their own right?
- Why are relationships between men and women as parents and partners so poorly understood and subject to so little rigorous attention?
- Why do we so often hide the suffering that we encounter behind a rational vocabulary of expertise?

Locating our current troubles

At the time of writing, care applications increase month on month and this has been happening since 2009 (CAFCASS, 2012). In the preceding year, 2008, the name of Peter Connolly became known as a result of the trial of the adults involved in his death. Reactions to this death followed a predictable pattern of focusing on what agencies (especially social workers) had or had not done. In an audit culture dominated by targets and timescales it was argued correctly, in our view, that social workers did not have the time to build the kinds of relationships that could support thoughtful assessments of risk. Others argued that social workers were too trusting of parents and, in this case, seduced by the mother's apparent compliance and that a more investigatory focus was needed. As time has gone by the views of those who espoused early removal appeared to achieve ascendancy as the increases in care demand suggest. Such increases are offered as evidence of timely, authoritative practice and of increasing and appropriate attention to the evidence of the harms done to children who are left 'too long' in abusive situations. Furthermore, adoption is being promoted as the optimal disposal for children who are removed.

In the commentary on the desirability of focused and timely removal, the following issues are rarely interrogated to understand their psychosocial underpinnings. Those who are removed are overwhelmingly economically and socially deprived. As Bywaters (forthcoming) notes, on 31 March 2012, a child living in Blackpool, England, was eight times more likely to be 'looked after' out of home – to be in the care system – than a child in Richmond upon Thames, an outer London borough. He demonstrates that this inequality in childhood chances exemplifies a pattern of difference across all English local authority areas which is systematically related to deprivation. However, this is not new. For years, researchers have noted that deprivation is the largest factor explaining major differences between local authorities in key aspects of child welfare, such as the proportion of children entering the care system (becoming 'looked after children',

LAC) or being subject to a child protection plan (CPP) (Bebbington and Miles, 1989; Oliver et al, 2001; Dickens et al, 2007).

A host of international evidence has poignantly demonstrated the consequences of removal for Aboriginal or first-nation communities (see, for example, Lonne et al, 2009). However, we would argue that while they may not seem as immediately visible they are evident in all impoverished communities where children are removed in disproportionate amounts or families are subject to other coercive state interventions. Thus we would suggest that when we hear the monthly roll call of statistics, we need to bear witness to the stories of loss and hurt, ambivalence as well as those of hope behind the statistics, stories that will echo and re-echo through the life histories of *all* those involved for years.

We argue for urgent attention to be paid to the role of poverty and deprivation not because they *cause* child abuse or because we believe that having wealthy parents secures a safe and happy childhood. Rather we are asserting that the radical individualisation of childhood limits the range of potential responses, creating a system which seeks an impossible actuarial certainty about risks to the relatively few, at the expense of proper help, or even proper conversations with the many adults and children who struggle and suffer occasionally or always.

The experiences of those trying to parent in a profoundly unequal society are not interrogated rigorously enough in current responses, with causation and correlation confused in a highly abstract language that renders real people and their practices invisible and/or unintelligible. For example, mental health difficulties, substance misuse and domestic abuse are advanced as central risk indicators for child abuse. However, they are not explored in the context of living with poverty and shame in an unequal society (see Chapters Two and Six). As Frost and Hoggett (2008) argue, psychosocial reactions to deprivation and shame are very important in understanding self-harm and harm to others. In the absence of rigorous discussion of the genesis of such harm, it is therefore not especially surprising that social work practices are often very poorly developed. For example, in the case of domestic abuse, interventions often appear marred by short-termism and authoritarianism. Thoughtful gender informed practice that disentangles the impacts of toxic attachments and feelings of stigma and shame are not common (Gibson, 2013). There is too often an emphasis on getting those who are acting violently removed from the family home or getting the 'victim' to leave. This short-term thinking is inimical to the kinds of humane family-minded practices we seek to advance in this book, and as we will argue, supports 'unsafe certainty' by contrast with the 'safe uncertainty' that we consider is needed (Mason, 2005; Hardham, 2006).

Intervening in families who are multiply deprived is wrought with dilemmas, which are profoundly moral and cannot be solely or simply understood through a language of expertise and technique. Currently, our social policies support the focus upon children within the politics of individual child rescue, and there appears to be little space to advance a politics of compassion or understanding towards their parents. Moreover, the role of wider family members such as grandparents, siblings and friendship networks in supporting children safely is often neither recognised nor supported properly. There also appears to be a profound neglect of the importance of place attachments for children and their families (Jack, 2010), which may have particularly serious consequences for those dealing with the consequences of rapid social change such as deindustrialisation and forced migration.

A muscular child protection project is not unknown in our history by any means and part of our project in this book is to locate the current settlement within the movement of ideas. In her moving recollections on a life in social work, Professor Olive Stevenson underscores the importance of history in ensuring ethical practice:

> I would like social workers to give a bit more time to history ... How did we get here? What has been gained or lost in the process? It sometimes seems to me that we are caught up in a dreadful world of happenings, crises and instant communication; this includes but goes far beyond our own share of child care alarms and excursions. There is a loss of collective wisdom, of a sense of continuity which gives a framework to understand current behaviour. (Stevenson, 2013: 97)

In the next section we present something of this chronicle and then consider how the landscape is currently being reworked.

Back to the future

Fox Harding (1997) outlined four value perspectives that have influenced child care policy and practice in the last decades: laissez-faire and patriarchy; state paternalism and child protection; the modern defence of the birth family and parents' rights; children's rights and child liberation. The following is a brief summary of each of these perspectives.

At the heart of the first perspective lies mistrust of the state and an acute awareness of the dangers of its powers. Domestic and family life, in particular, is seen as the realm of the private and should be left alone. From this perspective, the family is the one institution that has continued throughout history and still continues to undermine the state. The emphasis on the desirable separateness of the family from the power of the state appears to mean, in effect, that power in the family should lie where it is allowed to fall (Fox Harding, 1997: 11).

State paternalism and child protection is the name Fox Harding gives to the school of thought that favours extensive state intervention to protect children from poor parental care. Where parental care is inadequate, finding the child a new permanent home is favoured. The rights and liberties of parents are given a low priority; the child is paramount. This, we suggest, is the perspective today although reworked in a child-focused way as explored further later.

The modern defence of the birth family and parents' rights emphasises the importance of birth or biological families to both children and parents and these should be kept together where possible. The role of the state should be neither paternalist nor laissez-faire but supportive of families, providing the services they need to stay together. This perspective emphasises the importance of class, poverty and deprivation in explaining much of what occurs. It is an important genesis of family support and was a key influence on the Children Act 1989 although it has become more and more marginalised in policy and practice in the current context as we will argue throughout this book.

Finally, the fourth perspective identified by Fox Harding is that of children's rights and child liberation. This emphasises the importance of the child's own viewpoint and wishes, seeing the child as a separate entity with rights to autonomy and freedom. While the language of liberation has disappeared today, a child-focused perspective, discussed below, is increasingly central.

This classificatory system is valuable in clearly delineating particular value perspectives. As with all such classifications, however, lines are seldom drawn discretely and over time there has been leakage and further development. Gilbert et al (2011) note in their review of ten differing welfare regimes, including England, a transnational *child-focused* orientation. This orientation concentrates on the child as an individual with an independent relation to the state. It is not restricted to narrow concerns about harm and abuse; rather the object of concern is the child's overall development and wellbeing. This is evident in many of the countries' policies and programmes that target children as important means to advance the welfare state and levels of state expenditure (for example, New Labour governments from 1997–2010). These programmes seek to go beyond protecting children from risk to promoting children's welfare. Within a child-focused orientation, the state takes on a growing role for itself in terms of providing a wide range of early intervention and preventive services. This role represents the state's paternalistic interests in children's needs and wellbeing.

Although it borrows elements from both the child protection and family service orientations that were considered in previous work (Gilbert, 1997) to be the key classificatory perspectives internationally, Gilbert et al (2011) suggest that the child-focused orientation has a qualitatively different character and is shaped by two major, and somewhat contrasting, lines of influence. On the one hand, the child-focused orientation to social policy is influenced by ideas related to the 'social investment state' and on the other hand, it is influenced by the growing priority attached to 'individualisation'.

However, as Gilbert et al note, these two lines of influence do not sit easily together and can lead to tensions. The social investment approach is a future oriented perspective that considers children as worthy investments because of their potential in the future (see Fawcett et al, 2004: Lister, 2006). Gilbert et al argue that although investment in children involves a whole range of services, particularly those that will enhance prevention and intervention in problems at an early stage, these services are accompanied by an increased emphasis on regulating the behaviour of professionals, parents and children themselves. Regulation is designed to ensure that the investment in the early years pays off in the future. By contrast, the rationale for policies and practices that perceive children as individuals in the *here and now* concerns the quality of childhood. Here children are seen not so much as future workers but as future citizens as evidenced in the UN Convention on the Rights of the Child. Overall, despite the tensions between them, the child-focused orientation puts children's rights above parents' rights and emphasises parents' obligations as caregivers.

In this book we want to contribute to wider discussions that interrogate the notion of the individual that underpins *both* approaches (that is, investment and individualisation) and to argue for the importance of understanding children as well as adults as 'selves in relationships'. We argue for the importance of the notion of 'relational autonomy': this combines a concern for the individual's autonomy rights with an understanding of all family members as situated and engaged in relationships that are dynamic and multi-dimensional (see, for example, Choudry et al, 2010).

Under New Labour there was substantial spending on children in a social investment approach. The responsibilisation of their parents was accompanied by a significant expansion of resources with the emergence of programmes such as Sure Start. In the current climate of austerity, under a different government, matters are rather different with a sharper, more focused approach. Yes, the focus continues to be on children but within an even more time-limited project. While New Labour sought to reconstruct poor parents, the Coalition government established after the 2010 election at times appeared to have given up on them!

Parenting matters but not parents? Social investment meets child protection in an age of austerity

Social investment approaches feed in a toxic way into the state paternalism and child protection approach in England currently under the Coalition. All that matters is the child and parents need to shape up or the child will be shipped out. It is something of a paradox that, given the consensus that parenting matters, and indeed is the key element that makes a difference for children in similarly deprived circumstances, understanding parents as people and the meanings they attach to their practices seems to have such a low priority. Parents are seen as impacting upon children rather than being in relationships with them and with each other, thus practice focuses on how their actions/inactions do or do not affect children. A punitive ethos pervades practices often with parents (especially mothers) constructed as prioritising their own needs over those of their children.

There has been a focus on manualised parenting programmes and their virtues in an evidence-based paradigm. The discussions of technique, fidelity and validity further reinforce abstraction, removing us from the need for conversations with parents about what their lives are like, and what hopes and fears they have for themselves, their children and their relationships (see Chapters Six, Seven and Eight).

More generally, there is almost an acceptance that because adult service users fear the power of social workers, and/or because they are in denial about the harm they are causing children, they will be resistant to social workers. A very arid and one-dimensional portrayal of what are essentially social interactions between people in particular contexts emerges. This has not been helped by the relative paucity of large scale research into lived experiences of child protection processes. In recent years, important techniques have been promoted such as motivational interviewing to counter resistance (Forrester et al, 2007).

While we find such techniques extremely helpful, they need to be located within a broader engagement with ethical questions about how the current child protection system deals with multiply-deprived families in an unequal society and with the dynamics of shame and harm to self and others that flow from such inequalities. We also need a much more thoughtful understanding of resistance than is currently often to be seen in literature or practice. This understanding needs to be located within a broader understanding of the power social workers have and are recognised as having. This extends to being able to define both problems and responses. In a piece of research undertaken by one of the authors, exploring social care engagement with fathers, it was found that such fathers were often very concerned about the double standards that characterised practices. For example, it was often noted that if they were late for a contact visit, it was read by social workers as evidence of a lack of motivation. However, social workers were themselves often late for such visits. This was explained away by reference to traffic problems (Roskill et al, 2008).

In delivering talks on aspects of this book, we have often been accused of seeking to turn the clock back on decades of progress in understanding the needs of children and the risks posed by resistant and hostile parents. We are extremely chary of the idea that we have indeed had decades of progress. Indeed, while we are not postmodernists, we find the critique by postmodernists of assumptions that we are constantly progressing as human beings of value especially when we consider unintended consequences in child protection. To give one example, while it has seemed progress to get domestic abuse taken seriously by social workers, the cost has often been borne by women experiencing such violence when it is considered that they are not protecting their children adequately by continuing to endure it.

Ribbens McCarthy (2013) notes how a more generalised construction of childhood functions in a range of ways. She argues that the idealised notion of childhood as a time of protection and innocence in contemporary Western culture impedes the ability to acknowledge that all families are likely to be troubled, and fails to equip children to deal with such trouble when they encounter it, and indeed this failure may itself exacerbate the impact of trouble. She also notes the compelling evidence of different childhoods across time and space and of the importance of engaging with cultures and contexts. In so doing she engages head on with accusations of relativism.

We are aware that our own problematisation of current practice orthodoxies in this book may attract the accusation that we are relativising child abuse and neglect, and to an extent that is true. As we point out in the course of our arguments, there are some situations which are manifestly damaging to children and from which they must decisively be removed; however, there are many more where the whole family unit is suffering and where the additional suffering caused by removal of the child to all members of the family must properly be weighed and debated and a range of ameliorative options considered. Treating morally complex decisions as though they are morally simple, unfortunately, does not have the effect of making those decisions morally simple. We will argue that this illusion of simplicity can be an effect of the current child-centric (Hall et al, 2010) paradigm, particularly as we note in Chapter Five, when this is supported by selective invocation of 'hard science'. So, to the accusation that we teeter on the edge of the abyss of moral relativism and tolerance of child cruelty, we contend that fewer atrocities in the history of the world have happened as a result of equivocation than as a result of absolutism. Whereas tyranny is, or depends on absolutism, in a democratic polity we are, and must be, relativists in practice because we exercise judgement as citizens in shaping or finding ethical truth. Democratic and humane practice with disadvantaged families requires prudent judgement, and such judgement presupposes critical, even deconstructive, reflection on experience that is inherently contingent (Brown, 1994: 27).

In Brown's view, absolutism is the real danger not relativism. While Brown has referred more broadly to the political sphere, we might equally apply this in the more specific context of social work with children and families, and recognise the importance of a democratic and humane practice which takes account of varying perspectives, acknowledges different viewpoints and makes careful judgements about them. For this, we need a different, more debated and contested engagement with the problem of judgement. For example, Knorr-Cetina and Mulkay (1983) propose:

> The belief that scientific knowledge does not merely replicate nature *in no way* commits the epistemic relativist to the view that therefore all forms of knowledge will be equally successful in solving a practical problem, equally adequate in explaining a puzzling phenomenon or, in general, equally acceptable to all participants. Nor does it follow that we cannot discriminate between different forms of knowledge with a view to their relevance or adequacy in regard to a specific goal. (Knorr-Cetina and Mulkay, 1983: 6, emphasis added)

This position does not leave us bereft of moral standards. Rather, it asserts that these standards are not fixed and immutable but in the process of being continually renewed and reshaped within a given culture. While we may claim that child abuse is intrinsically wrong, it is clear that over the past 100 years our views about the nature and extent of the practice have undergone considerable change (Hacking, 1999). But this does not prevent the making of meaningful value judgements, made on the basis of 'contingent considerations', that is a careful appraisal of what is at stake, the possible alternatives and probable outcomes. This in turn means we must reanimate parents and children as people and this requires a different way of conceptualising practice.

Humane practice

> One third, more or less, of all the sorrow that the person I think I am must endure is unavoidable. It is the sorrow inherent in the human condition, the price we must pay for being sentient and self-conscious organisms, aspirants to liberation, but subject to the laws of nature and under orders to keep on marching, through irreversible time, through a world wholly indifferent to our well-being, toward decrepitude and the certainty of death. The remaining two thirds of all sorrow is homemade and, so far as the universe is concerned, unnecessary. (Aldous Huxley, *Island*)

It is imperative that social work acts to reduce the sorrow that is avoidable. Much has been written of the erosion of time and the distancing effects of current practice. Relationship based approaches have been promoted which are absolutely vital and there has been some acknowledgement of extending the ethic of recognition to parents (Turney, 2012). But the focus generally remains on the child, on entering the home to see the child, on inspecting the home to see the child is safe and has enough to eat. Danger is emphasised – danger of dogs, violence, of being lied to, of entering liminal spaces, no-go areas, places different and dirty. We are not dismissing danger and dirt but we do want to argue for the importance of understanding how 'othering' and distancing processes operate in unequal societies. As we explore more fully in Chapter Two a key insight from the ground breaking work of Wilkinson and Pickett (2009) on the consequences of the growth in inequalities in societies such as ours, concerns how distances between groups are intensified including between social workers and their service users. Within the past few decades, under both

Conservative and Labour administrations, greater distances emerged between individuals, groups and communities; these were physical and psychological and affected everyone. We will argue in this book that these processes of distancing contributed to a breakdown in feelings of solidarity and commonality in the face of vulnerability and adversity. Nowhere is such a breakdown more evident than in the rhetoric that politicians feel able and sometimes obliged to employ in relation to those who are receiving welfare benefits and/or those seeking asylum. This distancing has had pernicious effects on the relationship between child and family, social work and families themselves, and between the state and the intimate spaces of relationships.

We want to argue for a more sophisticated understanding of experience than is currently to be found in the literature. This requires critical distance on institutional categories, which have profoundly dehumanising effects.

> Social workers know how to inscribe everyday or mundane occasions as proper instances into institutional categories. Such inscriptive work quiets the tumultuous noise of drunken shouting between husband and wife. It cools out a child's hot tears. It manages the welts from a beating. Simply put, it modulates the noise, multiple dimensions and uncertainties of an immediately experienced reality. It substitutes regulated tonal symmetries provided through professional categories and texts for the noise of daily life. (de Montingny, 1995: 28)

That social workers can hear the noise of daily living is important in many respects. Viewed instrumentally from within the dominant child protection paradigm, hearing the noise is likely to lead to safer decisions. Knowing how the tones are modulated by significant events, by shifts in the relational context, by childbirth, by rows, by the developmental changes of childhood and adolescence, by death, simply means we can be more accurate in our predictions of future safety and harm. Our argument here, however, is that attending to the noise of everyday life is about more than this and allows us to undertake the necessary animation of the people and their interactions, to see them as members of our own species. Paraphrasing John Steinbeck in *Of Mice and Men*, 'knowing a person well never leads to hate and nearly always leads to love'; conversely, not knowing a person and seeing them only in instrumental terms and as means to an end (such as exploring their capacity to parent) may very well lead to indifference and cruelty.

We were vividly reminded of this when we were interviewing users of the advice and advocacy services run by Family Rights Group (Featherstone, Fraser, O'Dell et al, 2012). Julia cried as she explained that social workers had told her she was unable to have 'healthy' adult relationships as a result of a brief period in her care as a young child. Her child had been removed from her because it transpired her partner had a history of abuse that she had been unaware of. She had immediately separated from him and paid privately for counselling (as it was not available from the social worker who was concerned with the child's welfare only). Despite her actions, the child was placed in care while a risk assessment was carried out. No one seemed to have considered the ironies here. Would such a separation, for example, result in this child too being unable to have healthy adult relationships?

Another woman wept as she explained that she had not been supported as a mother by services that appeared to interpret their mandate in the narrowest child-centric terms. She had experienced a childhood of sexual abuse and had been in care. She had three children and had been subject to domestic violence from a partner that she had since separated from. When she found herself sinking into depression, she approached children's services for help and they made her children subject to a CPP, an action she described as 'bullying'. Indeed, she felt she had been bullied all her life, by her abusers and the services supposed to protect and support her. It is also important to note that not only were these women treated instrumentally but they were apparently left with little information about the very frightening processes they were being subject to, as we explore throughout this book.

In a powerful critique of the unfettered reign of scientific bureaucratic rationality in medicine, surgeon Miles Little (1995) makes a case for the place of the humanities in encouraging humane medicine. The arts demand an emotional response from the reader or audience, they shake up prejudices, they develop self-awareness and enhance understanding of the human condition. Characters are drawn with complexity, depicting love, loss, ambivalence, complicated motives, petty lies, profound deceits and the pernicious pull of destructive relationships.

> Novelists and poets persuade by over-powering reductionist scientific logic with another dimension of pluralist logic, and we respond with a feeling of truth identified and made manifest. This skill in persuasion is part of humanist communication, and it uses a logic different from that of science. There may be no scientific proof of what is said or revealed, but the revelation is no less 'true'. It expresses

the truth which resides in ethics, morality and aesthetics.
(Little, 1995: 166)

That we have to make such a case for social work with its origins in casework and the helping relationship is very much a sign of the times (Stevenson, 2013). As we discuss in Chapter Five, the politics of evidence has reached a high water mark, only what 'works' gets funded and the adjudications on the efficacy of various approaches are affected by hierarchies of evidence and are easily colonised by moral and ideological projects. These forces conspire to create a profound 'othering' of many of the families with whom social workers work. Too often we are too far away from what Raymond Williams (quoted in Frost and Hoggett, 2008) has called 'felt thoughtfulness': a capacity both to feel the pain of the other, even in their angry, violent or self-destructive enactments, and to think critically about the injustices that produce it.

This has not been an uplifting tale so far and, in our view, the current child protection system does not shine as an example of the sure march of progress. The ideals of reason and progress through dispassionate enquiry were laudable aims of modernity. As Bruno Latour notes: '[they were] for many decades our most cherished source of light, defended by giants, before [they] fell to the care of dwarfs' (1999: 300). In our view, these 'dwarfs' are fast colonising social work, which demands reason, emotion and, most of all, an intelligence that is disciplined *and* creative and is rooted in an understanding of our shared vulnerability and frailty as human beings. It is time to revitalise social work with children and families.

There is much to be fixed and many myths to shatter, but our argument in this book is an optimistic one. It does not have to be this way. Although he is fiercely critical of the status of morality in contemporary life, Alasdair MacIntyre (2007) sees the possibility of challenge to powerful elites and the superficial lustre of expertise in the ordinary activities of ordinary people:

> When recurrently the tradition of the virtues is regenerated, it is always in everyday life, it is always through the engagement by plain persons in a variety of practices, including those of making and sustaining families and households, schools, clinics, local forms of political community. And that regeneration enables such plain persons to put to the question the dominant modes of moral and social discourse and the institutions that find their expression in those modes. (MacIntyre 2007: xiii)

However, once a moral settlement is in place and the elites have claimed and colonised the moral space, there is a good deal of work to be done to get the conversations moving again. We hope that the chapters that follow will create the conceptual space to rehumanise social work with families and children. This requires a deep breath; the current child-centric discourse carries much moral weight, contributing we will argue to the 'diminution of the domain of public reasoning' (Sen, 2005: 157). Rather than empty out the moral and political aspects of experience: suffering, muddling through and getting by, coming through and breaking out, we want to fill them out and make them flesh.

Concluding remarks

In summary, we see the current child-centric risk paradigm as highly problematic ethically. It is wedded to constructions of children as individuals who are unanchored in networks and communities and operates with superficial understandings of the importance of attachments, histories and legacies. It does not adequately engage with how notions of belonging and identity are reworked across the life course. Moreover, we would suggest that the lack of a rich engagement with children's identities means practices are unlikely to succeed in gaining truthful accounts from children themselves of what is happening to them. Hence, they are likely to make them less safe. This is compounded by practice engagements that are mired in distance and individualism as social workers arrive in their cars from large remote offices at estates about which they have little knowledge and enter the homes of people about whose everyday lives they equally know little. Such visits take place within a Greek chorus that echoes and re-echoes in workers' inner and outer worlds. Children must be seen and talked to, bedrooms inspected and parents communicated with firmly from a perspective that understands they are likely to deny, minimise and be resistant. They are only here for the child.

We must ask are children really likely to talk to distant strangers? Are they likely to feel confident when they observe the disregard in which such strangers sometimes seem to hold their parents? Even when children's loyalties are profoundly compromised by their parents' abuse the possibilities for rich encounters are not supported by time limits and the lack of stability of the workforce. And here we encounter the viciousness of the circle within which we seem endlessly to turn. Social workers increasingly return from family visits to work in call centre type facilities lacking even a desk to call their own. Despite the recommendations of the Munro Review (2010) that a risk sensible ethos should pervade organisational cultures, they work in contexts that are often as inhumane as the practices families experience. Who can tell of fears, mistakes or anxieties in such contexts? It is little wonder that retention difficulties are such a chronic feature of the current landscape.

While we are clear that we do not have all the answers (or indeed many of them at all) we do seek to promote alternative models of practice in this book reaching back into our history to explore models such as patch based social work and making common cause with contemporary practices that are characterised by a commitment to team working and locally based family-focused approaches (see Chapters Seven and Eight). Overall, we seek to engage in dialogue and links with those who are developing a relational approach to welfare and safeguarding and contribute to a growing literature that calls for an alternative paradigm to that which is currently hegemonic (Cottam, 2013; Lonne et al, 2008; Melton, 2009).

Structure of the book

Chapter Two explores how welfare has been reshaped in the last decades as a transactional form came to reign in a society in love with the market. It explores the trajectory of child protection and borrows from a more general re-thinking of welfare states to begin to sketch out possibilities for a different settlement. Chapter Three argues for the importance of engaging with the work as an ethical project and the necessity of continuing moral conversations using a variety of perspectives. Chapter Four concerns itself with understanding both how evidence can be used to narrow down conversations and also to open them and again stresses the importance of debate rather than closure and orthodox thinking. Chapter Five explores the importance of developing a just culture in organisations so that the kind of social work we are promoting which places human beings and human factors at its heart can be developed. Chapter Six explores the lived experience of poverty and makes a case for social work practice that incorporates fully a recognition of the extraordinary power of ordinary help and strengthening the capacities of neighbourhoods and communities. Chapter Seven addresses neglected areas such as relationships between men and women as partners or expartners. We will argue that while parenting and parenting capacity are seen as critical in terms of impacting on children's welfare, an irony of the current policy and practice climate is how little attempt is made to understand parents themselves and their lives, what they want from each other, and for and from, their children. We take the issue of domestic abuse as an example. In Chapter Eight we argue that the notion of family as the context for the resolution of children's needs extends the scope for supporting change and reflects most children's lived experiences. We suggest barriers to family engagement in the care and protection of children have, in part, been a product of our reluctance to go beyond the presenting unit (however fractured that may be), despite the evidence that family networks are fluid, diverse and rarely geographically specific. Finally, in the concluding chapter, we pull our sundry threads together to offer a mosaic of possibilities for how we move forward together.

TWO

Re-imagining child protection in the context of re-imagining welfare

Something is profoundly wrong with the way we live today. For thirty years we have made a virtue out of the pursuit of material self-interest: indeed, this very pursuit now constitutes whatever remains of our sense of collective purpose. We know what things cost but have no idea what they are worth. (Judt, 2010: 1–2)

Introduction

Current policy responses to the economic crisis are mobilising social forces, including social work, in a divisive and authoritarian project against those most vulnerable. In the field of child protection, as indeed in other areas of welfare, the roots of current policies are to be found in those of previous New Labour administrations, but the trends pre-date them. From the late 1970s onwards, the doctrines of Reagan and Thatcher became dominant, promoting the virtues of letting the market rule in a triumph of neoliberalism. Although we recognise the term neoliberal is not a satisfactory one, as it is reductive, lumping together too many things, sacrificing attention to internal complexities and lacking in geo-historical specificity, we agree with Hall (2011) that there are enough common features to warrant using it.

Neoliberalism is in the first instance a theory of political economic practices that proposes that human well-being can best be advanced by liberating individual entrepreneurial freedoms and skills within an institutional framework characterized by strong private property rights, free markets, and free trade. The role of the state is to create and preserve an institutional framework appropriate to such practices. (Harvey, 2005: 2)

Across a range of countries, deregulation, privatisation and withdrawal of the state from many areas of social provision became common, transcending welfare regime typologies and encompassing states established after the collapse of the Soviet Union through to social democracies such as Sweden and New Zealand. A common feature across diverse systems was a rise in inequalities. In this context, it is important to note that from the late 19th century until the 1970s, the advanced societies of the West were becoming more equal. However, as Judt (2010: 13) noted, over the past 30 years 'we have thrown all this away'. This was not accidental, it was part of a determined political project.

Harvey (2005) noted the turnaround in the share of national income going to top income earners in a range of countries between the late 1970s and 1999. Extraordinary concentrations of wealth and power emerged in countries as diverse as Russia, Mexico, Latin America and China, with a similar process happening in the UK.

The work of epidemiologists Wilkinson and Pickett (2009) has illuminated the impact of this rise in inequality bringing an array of evidence in their book, *The spirit level: Why more equal societies always do better*, to reach important conclusions. They have collected internationally comparable data on health and a range of social problems: levels of trust, mental illness (including drug and alcohol addiction), life expectancy and infant mortality, obesity, children's educational performance, teenage births, homicides, imprisonment rates and social mobility. Their findings suggest that there is a *very strong* link between ill health, social problems and inequality. Differences in average income between whole populations or countries do not seem to matter beyond a certain level, but differences *within* those populations or countries matter greatly. The amount of income inequality in a country is crucial. Wilkinson and Pickett (2009) note strong findings from the data that levels of trust between members of the public are lower in countries where income differences are larger. For example, people trust each other most in the Scandinavian countries and the Netherlands, and least in very unequal countries such as the UK.

A linked insight from their work concerns how inequality *within* a society quite literally 'gets under the skin' of individuals leaving them feeling unvalued and inferior. They note the work of the sociologist Thomas Scheff (1988) who argued that shame is the key social emotion. 'Shame and its opposite, pride, are rooted in the processes through which we internalise how we imagine others see us' (Wilkinson and Pickett, 2009: 41). Greater inequality heightens our anxieties because it increases the importance of social status. We come to see social position as a key feature of a person's identity in an unequal society.

A range of other writers have explored compatible issues around the implications of unequal divisions in societies. Bourdieu's (1999) concept of social suffering drew attention to social misery, not just the unequal distribution of material goods but also people's lived experiences of domination and the accompanying feelings such as humiliation, anger, despair and resentment. Others have noted the implications of living in societies where there is, on the one hand, a growth in inequality with a corresponding silting up of social mobility and, on the other hand, a dominant belief that anyone can make it, and if you don't you are a loser (Frost and Hoggett, 2008). Here the work of symbolic interactionists such as Goffman (1968) is of value. Goffman described the social hurt of stigma: the experience of the individual who cannot produce the 'normal' social identity required and is aware that he or she does not come up to standard is that of being discredited and of a personal failure to pass. Because the opinion formed by those making judgements does not stop at presentation, but makes moral judgements and imputes certain characteristics, the discrediting of the person impinges on the whole identity. The stigmatised person shares the same belief system as the rest of the culture so the standards incorporated from the rest of society equip him/her to be aware of what others see as his/her failing, inevitably causing him/her to agree that they inevitably do fall short of what they really ought to be. Shame becomes a central possibility (Goffman, 1968: 18).

The past few decades saw enormous changes, not only in England itself as the Thatcher revolution in particular destroyed whole communities, but globally with movements of peoples that were unprecedented and often forced. It is vital to grasp the relationship between individual biographies and social processes such as those attached to huge social changes such as deindustrialisation and migration (Frost and Hoggett, 2008). During periods of rapid social change, powerless people become the objects of change rather than its agents. Deindustrialisation destroys whole communities and identities and there are considerable personal costs to forced migration. Frost and Hoggett (2008) note the importance of loss, grief and melancholia to understand the experiences of those whose communities are destroyed by processes of urban modernisation, or those who are the powerless objects of economic and social restructuring.

While Wilkinson and Pickett's (2009) methodology and findings have been contested, it is of interest how far across the political spectrum the concern with inequalities has ranged in recent years, from the former head of the IMF and the *Economist* magazine to the OECD (see for example, OECD, 2011). This concern has been motivated by diverse fears. For example, neoliberals themselves recognise their promise of social mobility through hard work is threatened through the silting up of opportunity. Others fear for the future of democracy, especially in the US where big money and political influence seem to be in a toxic embrace. There has also been concern that the growth in inequality fuelled the borrowing (especially subprime borrowing in housing) that contributed to the economic crisis.

For the authors, alongside the issue of shame, a key insight from Wilkinson and Pickett (2009) concerns how distances between groups are intensified, including between social workers and their service users. Within a couple of decades, under both Conservative and Labour administrations, greater distances emerged between individuals, groups and communities; these distances were physical and psychological, and affected everyone including service users and social workers. We will argue in this book that the processes of 'othering' families and individuals in adversity are having a profound and pernicious effect on the relationship between child and family, social work and families themselves, and between the state and the intimate spaces of relationships.

Neoliberalism, risk and responsibility

As Culpitt (1999: 35) notes, under neoliberalism social policy successfully eclipsed the former moral imperatives of mutual obligation that sustained political support for welfare states. A new rhetoric of governance argued for the lessening of risk, not the meeting of need. This is of considerable importance as a diverse cast of people and issues became known only through the language of risk. Indeed, Kemshall (2002) noted social work shifted from a preoccupation with need to one of risk, and Webb (2006) argued that need and risk became conflated with social work taking on a role in risk regulation and as expert mediator for problematic populations and vulnerable people. Webb (2006) noted an ambivalence here which was manifest through instrumental rationality in terms of calculating and regulatory practices, and substantive rationality in securing personal identity through dialogic and expressive face work. That ambivalence was to be sharply posed from 2008 onwards when research findings exposed how far instrumental rationality had won the day in the context of publicity surrounding the death of Peter Connolly (White et al, 2010).

Culpitt (1999) argued that under neoliberalism the notion of responsibility was deconstructed from any social nexus:

> The disadvantaged individual has come to be seen as potentially and ideally an active agent in the fabrication of their own existence. Those 'excluded' from the benefits of a life of choice and self-fulfilment are no longer merely the passive support of a set of social determinations: they are people whose self-responsibility and self-fulfilling aspirations have been deformed by the dependency culture, whose efforts at self-advancement have been frustrated for so long that they suffer from 'learned helplessness', whose self-esteem has been destroyed. And it thus follows, that they are to be assisted not through the ministrations of solicitous experts proffering support and benefit cheques, but through their engagement in a whole array of programmes for their ethical reconstruction as active citizens. (Rose, 1996, quoted in Culpitt, 1999: 36–37)

Thus those who were poor were active agents in their own poverty and, moreover, their poverty was to become transformed into an indicator of risk in relation to themselves or others. In many welfare regimes, the role of the state become reconstructed as that of offering them tools to transform themselves as explored below.

Successive Conservative governments of the 1980s and 1990s, with their free market passions, did not, in the main, spend on programmes to reconstruct 'active citizens'. There was a conflict between the economic liberals and traditional authoritarians within Conservatism in relation to the role of the state, but neither strand saw the role in a way that New Labour was to. Economic liberals emphasised individual autonomy and the unfettered right of the market, and this clashed with that of the traditional authoritarian who wanted a strong role for the state with a commitment to law and order, nationhood and the policing of behaviours particularly in relation to those that might destabilise the two parent family. As Fox Harding (1999) noted, in practice there was some accommodation of the conflicting ideologies. Libertarian Conservatism supported laissez-faire economics and a strong state to maintain traditional and family values.

It was New Labour, elected in 1997, that really took on the project of reconstructing active citizens. Rustin (2008) has argued that an under-recognised difference between the era of Thatcherism and that of New Labour lies in the theoretical frameworks which justified the two projects. The Thatcherites were inspired by free market economists such as Milton Friedman and Hayek. For these economists, sociology was their enemy as it highlighted concerns about inequality and social injustice. Because New Labour was also so committed to the market, its reliance on a different disciplinary underpinning has been less obvious. Its most influential theorist was Giddens, a sociologist. Of importance has been the choice of 'globalisation' as the central idea through which thinking has been organised and the occlusion of capitalism occurred.

> Globalization is seen as a system of expanded economic competition, to which all national economies, including Britain's, are increasingly exposed. It is also seen as a system of communications which is transforming life-worlds, dissolving old collective identities (such as those of class or community) and engendering new and more individualized identities of subjects, as consumers, 'active citizens' and the like. New Labour's programme has been one of adaption to these proclaimed new realities, with the necessity to compete in global markets, and to respond to the demands of new individual subjects for choices in as many spheres of life as possible, as its major guideline. (Rustin, 2008: 275)

Giddens (1998) argued that in place of the welfare state, a social investment state needed to be constructed. The key guideline was 'investment in *human capital*, wherever possible, rather than the direct provision of economic maintenance' (Giddens, 1998: 117, emphasis in original). While the old welfare state sought to protect people from the vagaries and inevitable risks posed by the market, a social investment state sought to facilitate the integration of people into the market. People's security comes not from the role played by the state but from their capacity to re-skill themselves. The state spends not to enable individuals to exist in the here and now but to ensure the spending has a pay-off:

> The notion is that such investments will be more suited to the labour markets of global capitalism, in which job security is rare, and flexibility is highly valued. For its part, social policy should be 'productivist' and investment oriented rather than distributive and consumption oriented. The emphasis in social policy should shift from consumption and income maintenance programs to those that invest in

people and enhance their capacity to participate in the productive economy. (Jenson and Saint-Martin, 2001: 5)

This was a future-oriented and child-focused project: spending could be legitimately directed to supporting and educating children *especially in their early years* because they hold the promise of the future. Early spending would insure against future risks, such as those of criminality, poor health, unemployability. An instrumental approach to their parents emerged in that they were constructed primarily as conduits to ensuring children's welfare. A key responsibility was to engage in paid work, both in order to support themselves and their children, but also to provide the right type of environment in which their children could grow up. Indeed, this is of great relevance to discussions about the child protection system, while a discourse around child poverty was mobilised and legitimated, it was routinely disassociated from a rigorous discussion of the poverty of their parents (Lister, 2006). This reinforced and further facilitated discourses which did not consider adult poverty a matter of concern (except, to some extent, in relation to pensioners).

Ambitious programmes such as Sure Start were all funded centrally and rolled out nationally. These were concerned to create easily accessible preventative provision that sought to help families develop their skills in developing pathways out of poverty and social exclusion. They drew on US evidence in relation to the future cost savings to be gained by investing early in children. They were also concerned to counter the suspicion that was seen as attached to older services such as social work. David Blunkett, the then Home Secretary, spoke when launching the Sure Start programme of wanting to "do something that would be entirely new and innovative from the word go, to get to the core of the difficulties facing families and communities" (quoted in Gardner, 2002: 35). He argued that one of the difficulties was the deep cynicism about professionalism and about government in all its guises. It also became apparent at that time that there was a strong sense among policy makers that Sure Start was a necessary development in view of the 'failure' of Social Service departments (although the exact nature of the failure was left unspecified).

As Frost and Parton (2009: 65) noted, the emphasis under New Labour seemed to shift from the earlier universal emphasis embodied by Sure Start towards a more muscular interventionist stance targeted at those deemed 'hard to reach'. By 2005, through the Respect Agenda, a high profile focus emerged on anti-social families. The families with chronic levels of risk who were considered to present high costs to society became the new focus of policy concern. Indeed it was argued that 4% of families presented multiple, complex needs and were not responsive to existing programmes. 'Think Family' as the primary policy response sought to bring together previously segregated service arrangements (adult services and children's services) and develop a holistic approach to families with complex and enduring needs (Morris and Featherstone, 2010). Within this policy stream were initiatives such as Family Intervention Projects, Family Nurse Partnerships and Family Pathfinders. The policy discourses surrounding these initiatives identified such families as failing but primarily failing to access and utilise the change opportunities presented by the various prevention programmes such as Sure Start (Morris and Featherstone, 2010).

Safeguarding, child protection and New Labour

The Children Act 1989 was a comprehensive piece of legislation that drew on decades of research and extensive consultation with an array of stakeholders. In its concern to ensure that children were protected and that they were able to remain within their families wherever possible, it brought in significant new provisions. It signalled the potential to move from 'all or nothing' service responses to family support becoming a key part of the service response. Accommodation in some form of state care could be used flexibly as part of a package for example.

It is important to note that the legislation was underpinned by an ethos of partnership working with parents and families. While a slippery concept, the partnership notion at its best signalled the importance of sharing information and trying to achieve co-operation and consensus. However, as study after study has shown, this has proven very difficult in practice. Immediately prior to New Labour coming into office, *Messages from research* (Department of Health, 1995), in its extensive review of the Children Act 1989, had urged a refocusing of professional practice based upon evidence of parental alienation as a result of suspicious risk averse interventions.

Under New Labour, safeguarding became the term used to signal a broader more ambitious remit for children's services than that encompassed in child protection. Safeguarding not only encompassed the need to pay attention to harms to children not usually considered, such as bullying or traffic accidents, but also was located within a broader project concerned with tackling social exclusion. The term 'family support', used since the Children Act 1989, and the subject of considerable debate throughout the 1990s, was subsumed within a broader language of intervention and prevention. However, over the New Labour period, a number of child deaths and the attendant publicity (in particular, that of Victoria Climbié) continued to ensure that the risks to children of being harmed by their parents or carers retained very strong purchase in the popular imagination, and in practice meant that a set of activities associated with 'child protection' were central to the work of social workers in local authorities.

Lonne et al (2009) identify the main features of a child protection paradigm that they consider dominant across many countries. The term child protection, rather than, for example, child welfare or supporting families, is used; the focus is on the assessment of risk to children by family and caregivers; services tend to be managerialised with priority given to procedures and risk averse practices; the referral portal tends to be one in which reports and referrals are for children at risk rather than for child or family in need; many countries have mandatory reporting protocols; prevention and family support are in the policies but are secondary to the primary role of child protection (Lonne et al, 2009: 3-4).

In practice, New Labour maintained an uneasy and complex mix of child protection, and a broader focus on social exclusion and children's outcomes in a version of the child-focused orientation outlined by Gilbert et al (2011) as explored in Chapter One. This mix was subsumed within a particular mode of governance as we explore in Chapter Five, with a veritable panoply of command and control techniques put in place.

It may seem ironic that given an initial scepticism about the state, New Labour ended up being associated with an overweening state, or is it? Did the scepticism lead to the freneticism? Was New Labour a project rooted in distrust of the public sector? Certainly, its hyperactive emphasis on embracing the 'new' alongside the proliferation of audit left many citizens, including social workers and service users, fearful and disoriented.

While programmes such as Sure Start opened up possibilities for a more solidaristic and universalist approach to risk (need having been eclipsed), there was a more worrying underbelly. Indeed, we would argue, New Labour created the conditions for the perfect storm of today; catch them early, focus on children, treat parents either instrumentally or render them invisible, and identify and treat the feckless and risky. While they were spending money, the consequences were not quite so obvious. However, under the Coalition government and its enforced austerity, matters are rather different. This residualism requires that parents be held to blame for their own predicaments, and has increasingly involved the conscription by policy makers of a range of 'expert' discourses to validate increasingly unforgiving and interventionist practices in relation to (primarily poor) families.

Responding to crisis

> New Labour's story – of self-responsible individuals realising their potential through projects with chosen others, in a modern, flexible economy, adapting better to globalisation than its continental neighbours, and served by modern, businesslike government agencies and services – was tired and discredited by the time of the 2010 election. (Jordan and Drakeford, 2012: 11)

As Rustin (2008) noted, there were systemic contradictions which New Labour proved either uncaring about or unable to engage with, and these are currently the subject of sustained reflection among a diverse set of constituencies. These were levels of inequality as explored above in the work of Wilkinson and Pickett (2009). The lack of concern with the gaps between groups in society by leading New Labour figures such as Blair and Mandelson has been interrogated in the context of social scientific evidence of the implications at such an array of levels. Other linked contradictions cohere around the crisis of social solidarity with the social response to this diminished solidarity, evident in moral panics and periodic outburst of hysteria against perceived threats to security and wellbeing. Finally, a third systemic contradiction concerns the environmental crisis.

It is interesting that the Conservative party came to the general election of 2010 with a programme focused on engaging with some of these contradictions. While now apparently out of favour, the work of Philip Blond (2010), outlined in his book *Red Tory*, seemed to have some influence certainly on David Cameron. Blond argued that monopoly capitalism, as much as the power of the centralising state, had been responsible for a damaging weakening of civil society. Economic liberalism and social liberalism needed combating. The combination of these led to a lethal mix of neoliberal markets and oppressive state. He argued for intermediate organisations between the individual and the market and the individual and the state, supporting co-operative production and social enterprises. The market needed moralising through the combating of monopolies and development of mutualist structures of ownership and reward. The public sector needed transforming into a civil state through employee ownership, active participation and public engagement, social enterprises, cooperatives and local financial institutions.

Another influence was contained in the work of the Centre for Social Justice, which argued that Britain had become broken as a result of New Labour's individualistic and contractual model. It had weakened social bonds, community and mutuality, excluded a poor minority and led to the political alienation of the younger generation. The existing benefits system trapped claimants; marriage and saving should be rewarded; people doing small amounts of paid work should benefit from it (see www.centreforsocialjustice.org.uk).

However, there has been a rapid shift from the pre-election softer focus exemplified by Cameron's injunction to 'hug a hoodie', with a much sharper and nastier focus over time with cuts to welfare taking on totemic significance and increasingly strident rhetoric against the 'shirkers' who are counterpoised to the virtuous 'strivers'. This divisiveness forms, in the authors' view, a key backdrop to work with families and needs to be constantly reflected upon when considering current policy directions.

The focus on early intervention began under New Labour and has been sharpened under the Coalition. This is a future-oriented project building on elements of social investment and moral underclass discourses. It incorporates an unforgiving approach to time and to parents – improve quickly or within the set time limits. As we argue in Chapter Four, it is shored up by a particularly potent neuroscientific argument, which has been widely critiqued from within neuroscience itself (Bruer, 1999; Uttal, 2011) but is unchallenged in current policy. Read carefully, the *original* neuroscience literature shows that the infant brain has quite remarkable resilience and plasticity when exposed to ordinary patterns of 'chaotic' neglect usually seen in the population referred to children's social care (Wastell and White, 2012). In truth, if changes to the brain were the criterion for removal from parents, very few children would be removed.

Initially, the commissioning of Professor Eileen Munro by the Coalition government to review the 'child protection system' seemed to exemplify an interest in establishing a 'new' direction after the command and control tyranny of New Labour. And indeed the recommendations departed in very important and welcome respects from previous approaches, with their concern to reduce prescription and an emphasis on a learning culture through the promotion of a systems approach to child deaths for example (Munro, 2011).

There is ample evidence that despite government statements that it welcomed the recommendations and would implement most of them, matters have moved in a very different direction indeed. There are a number of key elements to the current approach: the continuation of a risk–averse approach especially in relation to removing children early and the promotion of adoption. The focus is the individual child, who needs protecting from an array of harms which are often explicitly located in the failings or omissions of parents. Indeed, there is now no official recognition that parents should be engaged with as resources for their children. For example, in the rewritten guidance *Working Together* (DfE, 2013), there is a conspicuous failure throughout the document to acknowledge children as members of families or communities and to stress the importance of social workers working in partnership with families when children are in need and at risk of harm. At the time of writing the Children and Families Bill is explicitly focused on speeding up court decision making and adoption.

Indeed we would argue that we now have an up–to–date child–focused version of the 'state paternalism and child protection' perspective described by Fox Harding (1997) that seeks to rescue children and equip them for a world that is thoroughly saturated in the values of the market. As Kirton (2013) notes, the focus of adoption fits well with a neoliberal emphasis, offering a largely privatised solution to the consequences of social problems. It is the epitome of individualised responses premised upon construction of children as unfettered individuals rather than as relational beings. We would argue that it is difficult to overstate the impact that adoption without consent has on the system as a whole. It is unavailable in many other jurisdictions and its availability here reinforces the temporal pressures on decision makers and artificially delimits consideration of support for whole families.

Re-imagining welfare and re-imagining child protection

In a very interesting article Levitas (2012a) argues against reading 'Big Society' discourses and discourses around austerity solely through a 'hermeneutics of suspicion' and the need for a 'hermeneutics of faith' drawing from Ricoeur. This is necessary, she argues, because of the need to understand why discourses of austerity and the 'Big Society' have purchase among those whose interests are not served by Coalition policy.

Levitas (2012a) notes the need to understand why, for 200 years, working class self–organisation was a fundamental part of the collective provision against risk. A vast array of organisations fostered and supported such self organisation from the Methodist Church, through the Trade Union movement and the Co-operative Women's Guild with middle class involvement also. These forms of self-organisation have changed with time and place but have not disappeared. A hermeneutics of faith insists there is something real here that the Big Society speaks to, although it is ironic that the Tories do not accept how much was eroded through the policies pursued under Thatcher when relatively stable work-based communities were destroyed. New Labour's accommodation to globalisation meant that success equated to moving on and out of communities.

Levitas argues that austerity too needs to be read through a hermeneutics of faith for ecological reasons. We cannot go on growing indefinitely – there have to be limits set. She argues that reading the Big Society and austerity through a hermeneutics of faith takes us away from critique towards a more utopian method of considering an alternative future. By utopia is meant the expression of a desire for a better way of living and being, a desire braided through human culture. She argues that utopia as method has three modes. The first is archaeological, piecing together the images of the good society that are embedded in political programmes, and social and economic policies. The second is an ontological mode which addresses the question of what kind of people particular societies develop and encourage. What is understood as human flourishing, what capabilities are valued, encouraged and genuinely enabled, or blocked and suppressed by specific existing or potential social arrangements? The third is an architectural mode – that is, the imagination of potential alternative scenarios for the future, acknowledging the assumptions about and consequences for the people who might inhabit them. These in turn must be subject to archaeological critique, addressing the silences and inconsistencies all such images must contain, as well as the political steps forward that they imply:

> To read reduced consumption and the Big Society through a hermeneutics of faith is to create a narrative in which they cease to be an ideological cover for neo-liberal dispossession of the poor, and become positive attributes embedded in another potential society. The utopian approach asks the questions, what are the economic and social conditions under which these ideas would cease to be repressive, moralizing claptrap? The answer involves seven key principles: rethinking what counts as production and wealth, and measuring what matters; making sustainability central; prioritizing human flourishing and well-being; promoting

> equality; addressing the quality of work; revaluing care.
> (Levitas, 2012a: 336)

These seven principles could offer some help in re-imagining child protection but they need to be specifically interrogated and located within our understandings of how we comprehend the notion of the 'individual' child. At the heart of this book is a critique of policies that promote the child simply as an individual unanchored in place and with an identity that can be reconstructed at will, without a need to reference past connections. These are children from specific places, places that have already been subject to processes of loss at a range of levels. As the analysis from Paul Bywaters (forthcoming) has demonstrated graphically, place matters in a world saturated by regional inequalities. As noted in Chapter One, his analysis shows for example that, on 31 March 2012, a child living in Blackpool, England, was eight times more likely to be 'looked after' out of home – to be in the care system – than a child in Richmond upon Thames, an outer London borough. This inequality in childhood chances exemplifies a pattern of difference across all English local authority areas which is systematically related to levels of deprivation. He also notes the longstanding evidence that that deprivation is the largest factor explaining major differences between local authority areas in key aspects of child welfare, such as the proportion of children entering the care system (becoming 'looked after' children) or being subject to a child protection plan.

Children are not simply 'individuals' in a neoliberal fantasy of unfettered market actors. Across a range of disciplines from psychology to philosophy to the sciences, the recognition has emerged of our profound interdependence as human beings. To think of a child as a free floating individual denies elemental ties; to the body that gave birth to her, the breast that fed her, the aunt who sneaked her sweets, the streets where she played, the friends she played with. Interdependence is the basis of human interaction and autonomy and independence are about the capacity for self-determination rather than self-sufficiency. Vulnerability is part of the human condition and the experience of vulnerability varies contextually and temporally. No one is just a giver or receiver of care. Care is an activity binding everyone. Indeed as Williams (2001) argues, recognition of the importance of care and interdependence can open up possibilities for re-imagining welfare. The starting point is recognition of care of the self and others as meaningful activities in their own right, involving everyone – men and women, old and young, able-bodied and disabled. In giving and receiving care, everyone can, in the right conditions of mutual respect and material support, learn the civic responsibilities of responsibility, trust, tolerance for human limitation and frailties, and acceptance of diversity. Care is part of citizenship. Moral worth is attributed to key dimensions of caring relationships, such as dignity and the quality of human interaction, whether based upon blood, kinship, sexual intimacy, friendship, collegiality, contract, or service. Moreover, diversity and plurality in the social process of care is respected and recognised.

Inequalities in care giving and care receiving are exposed through questioning who benefits and who loses from existing policies. Inequalities may be constituted through different relations, particularly gender, but also disability, class, occupational status, age, ethnicity, race, nationality, religion, sexuality, and marital status. Care requires time, and financial and practical support, while quality, affordability, accessibility, flexibility, choice, and control are key to services based on inclusive citizenship where all involved in the processes of care have a voice. Care is not only personal but also an issue of public and political concern whose social dynamics operate at local, national, and transnational levels:

> The reprivatisation of care services, in conditions of women's increased participation in paid work, has intensified national and international forms of gendered exploitation constituted especially through class, 'race'/ethnicity and migrant status. (Williams, 2001: 488)

The care literature rests on an understanding of human beings that is profoundly relational. The notion of 'independence' is but a fantasy that is based upon denial of our interdependence in a world that is fragile and needs to be sustained both emotionally and physically.

In the delivery of services, the notion of relational welfare has emerged as a counterpoint to what was considered the 'transactional' welfare model of New Labour and the New Right. It eschews the idea of welfare as a business involving transactions between customer and service provider not only because it cannot capture the nature of the exchange, but also in trying to do so, it corrupts it and diminishes the wider society, reinforcing the fracturing and dislocation that is so prevalent as a result of neoliberal social policies and a target driven audit obsessed culture. Cottam (2011: 134–5) outlines the key features of relational welfare. She starts with the scale of the challenges facing the post-war model. First, there is a mismatch between the services on offer and the needs of the population. At the same time as the services on offer have seemed to be increasingly out of step with wider society and current needs, the demands have been increasing relentlessly. The reforms that have been tried have rarely improved outcomes and have often made things worse. The market reforms have intensified a transactional relationship where what is actually wanted is something more human, caring and time rich.

Cottam explores what a relational model might look like. She notes that key features of a number of emergent new approaches are: the intensive use of distributed systems; blurred boundaries between production and consumption; an emphasis on collaboration; and a strong role for personal values and mission. She offers an example from the work done by the organisation Participle. Participle takes entrenched social problems and develops new solutions that can scale nationally.

> As part of this work we live alongside those whom we are working with – the young, the elderly … families suffering from entrenched deprivation: financial, social and psychological. These are families who have previously been hardest to support, and with whom we see these new relational approaches working. (Cottam, 2011: 137)

Cottam offers the example of Ella, who is a mother within one of the 'troubled families' targeted by the Coalition and previously by New Labour. She argues that the family manifest the breakdown between the state and the citizen – visited by an endless stream of different workers who are both called upon by the family as well as 'intervening'.

> The constant visits and delivery of messages do not constitute a conversation, and the family do not feel properly listened to or understood. Asked to change, they have no lived experience of what this might feel like; and, worse still, they know that these commands are accompanied by the dead weight of expectation that they can't change – 'this family will never change', it was explained to us. (Cottam, 2011: 138)

Furthermore from the perspective of the workers, the system constraints were devastating. Eighty six per cent of their time was spent on system driven tasks with only 14 per cent in direct contact, but even that percentage was problematic with dialogue dictated by the forms and their need for data and information. 'The system is a costly gyroscope that spins round the families, keeping them at the heart of the system, stuck exactly where they are' (Cottam, 2011: 139).

So what was done? Families got to choose their worker and decide who was actually in a position to support them and the ratio of 86 to 14 was reversed. In choosing those they wanted to work with them, mothers such as Ella chose professionals who would neither be 'soft' or those they saw as dehumanised – they chose those who confessed they did not necessarily have the answers but who convinced them they would 'stick with it'. What they offered was driven by human qualities rather than rule books and there was a lack of reliance on jargon. A small amount of money was made available to the families themselves to identify which services they would find helpful. Workers used a range of approaches and were supported by supervision that recognised the emotional complexity of the work.

When outlining their philosophy, there are many synergies with the strengths based approaches found in an international family support literature (Dolan et al, 2006). The focus on capabilities (derived from the very influential work of Amartya Sen) is crucial – professionals are not there to intervene and solve problems – they are there to listen, challenge and support a process of discovery and transformation. Relationships are of course key: within and between families; between families and the team; with neighbours and wider communities.

Further re-imagining is found in the work of Jordan and Jordan (2000). They argued very presciently that New Labour could not seem to move beyond attempts to hold parents responsible for their children's upbringing and beyond propping up the creaky structure of family life. When parents were not able to do what was required, Tony Blair began the focus on adoption which is now fully flowering under the Coalition.

We suggest, following the lead set by Jordan and Jordan (2000) well over a decade ago, the need for a project that involves the following: thinking beyond individuals, supporting the capacity of families to care, recognising and building the capacities of communities, using state service such as foster parents and periods in good quality care in imaginative ways, and also as part of widening opportunities and responsibilities. These points are returned to throughout this book.

Conclusion

In the current climate, social work faces a choice – to be part of authoritarian demonisation or to offer hope and support to families to care safely and flourish. In order to do the latter, it needs to escape the shackles of individualistic and mechanistic ways of working. Moreover, it needs to abandon a belief in its essential innocence and to recognise its history under all sorts of highly problematic political regimes. The dominant child protection paradigm fits within a highly individualistic approach to families and, in essence, is compatible with a neoliberal emphasis on individual solutions to what are public troubles manifesting in private pain and sorrow.

THREE

We need to talk about ethics

[C]hild protection raises complex moral and political issues which have no one right technical solution. Practitioners are asked to solve problems every day that philosophers have argued about for the last two thousand years. ... Moral evaluations can and must be made if children's lives and well being are to be secured. What matters is that we should not disguise this and pretend it is all a matter of finding better checklists or new models of psychopathology – technical fixes when the proper decision is a decision about what constitutes a good society. (Dingwall et al, 1983: 244)

Written 30 years ago, this closing paragraph of a lucid ethnography of social work by sociologists Robert Dingwall and Topsy Murray and socio-legal scholar John Eekelaar underscores the moral and ethical aesthetic at the core of practice. Unfortunately, their wise counsel was not followed and social work has been mired in a series of technical fixes which have distracted us from, and masked, the moral nature of the work. Thus, the right debates have not taken place, or at least have not taken place in the right spaces.

This chapter seeks to return to Dingwall et al's imperative and explores both the importance, and the precariousness, of ethics in a risk averse context. Following procedures remains a central professional imperative and there has not been a debate at a societal level for some time about the value base that should underpin the work. We draw from a range of writings to urge the importance of supporting processes that ensure multiple voices can be heard and multiple forms of 'suffering' recognised. We argue for dialogic processes to be part of social work's day-to-day practices and for a wider commitment to public dialogue about the means and ends of practices.

Hollowing out ethics?

Ethical propositions are statements of value related to action.
... Value-statements may draw on abstract or ideal notions but at the same time they necessarily carry with them

implications for the way in which individuals act and the
relationship between people as members of social groups.
(Hugman and Smith, 1995: 2)

A number of writers have noted the lack of ethical debate about the
nature of practice interventions in child protection but we would add
also that it is vital to understand and locate these practices in the context
of the overall purpose of the work which has been little debated. Lonne
et al (2009: 114) argue that moral concern about risk to children and
outrage about 'bad' or 'dangerous' parents and the failure of professionals
to avert child deaths and injury has driven practice rather than ethical
debate about the nature of these interventions. Webb (2006) argues
that, in a context where a preoccupation with knowing and eliminating
risk has hollowed out the social work project, the moral identity of the
social worker has come adrift and needs to be recast.

It has been argued that the absence of discussion about ethics is
perhaps because it is too hard to find an ethical framework that could be
applied to such a contested area and across such a range of jurisdictions,
disciplines and legislative arrangements and cultures (Lonne et al, 2009).
However, we consider that the absence of overt discussion is linked to
an acceptance that the aims and means have been settled and that there
is consensus about the following issues. The task is about protecting
'the child' from an ever expanding array of harms with parents and
other family members constructed as means rather than ends. By this
we mean they are constructed as means towards the realisation of, or
obstruction of, children's protection rather than people who are worthy
of consideration in their own right. The possibility of complexity in
relation to the needs and interests of different stakeholders is often
left unaddressed as well as the wider implications of who is being
intervened with and removed. There is a profound and problematic
confusion about time and temporality – get children out early but
the long-term consequences are left unaddressed for all. Social work
involvement may pass in the blink of an eye, but the family may be left
coping with the consequences for generations. As discussed in previous
chapters, the perspective fits with the value perspective identified by
Fox Harding (1997) as 'state paternalism and child protection' which
was dominant through the 1970s and 1980s and the child-focused
orientation identified by Gilbert et al (2011).

We agree with Webb (2006) that locating ethical discussions in a
wider interrogation of risk is crucial for a number of reasons. The
desire by the public for certainty and 'omni-competence' on the
part of central and local authorities has been evident in a range of

domains but one of the most high profile areas has been social work with children who are considered to be at risk of harm. In particular, media coverage of 'atrocity tales' (Best, 1990) has been shown over the decades to influence policy directions in a wide range of countries and has contributed to a climate where there has been a decline in trust in expert systems alongside a continued insistence that risks can be detected and eliminated (see Gilbert et al, 2011). A further and really important issue is the way need has become reconstructed as risk. Thus, for example, poverty becomes framed as evidence of individual deficit in a neoliberal project. Poor parents are poor because of their own character flaws and are also putting their children at risk.

Exploring different schools of ethics: an overview

In discussions of ethics currently, we note pleasing evidence of the need to consider what a whole field of thinkers *over many centuries* can contribute to thinking. We agree with Houston (2010) who argues that ethical pluralism is inevitable, given the multiple nature of social life. It is, therefore, of value to outline the different theories that exist (see the edited collection by Gray and Webb, 2010). Deontology is an ethical theory deriving from the philosophy of Kant. This emphasises individual autonomy and choice, and is concerned with guiding individuals to make the right choices through understanding moral duties, obligations, rules and principles. Teleology refers to those ethical theories that are concerned with ultimate purposes or end states such as utilitarianism and consequentialism. Utilitarianism holds that given a number of possible courses of action, the one chosen should be the one that will be of most benefit to the greatest number. Consequentialism refers to the theory that gives weight to the consequences of our actions and moral decisions.

In social work the seven principles of casework, outlined by Biestek in 1957, have been surprisingly influential as ethical codes though, as Banks (1995) highlights, they were not intended as such but rather as pointers towards good practice. The principles were as follows: individualisation; purposeful expression of feelings; controlled emotional involvement; acceptance; non-judgmentalism; client self-determination; and confidentiality. A key theme running through these principles – and subsequent additions – was respect for the individual person as a self-determining being (Banks, 1995). Banks notes that although Biestek did not include it in his list, his principles are compatible with it. Respect for persons is rooted in the categorical imperative formulated by Kant: 'So act as to treat humanity, whether in your own person or that of any other, never solely as a means but always also as an end' (Banks, 1995: 28). The individual is worthy of respect simply because he or she is a person, regardless of what he or she has done, or whether he or she is useful to others. This approach fits within the deontological approach concerned with the rules that should be followed irrespective of consequences.

Criticisms of Biestek and his underling principles have been wide-ranging and longstanding. An important critique emerged in the 1970s with the development of radical/Marxist approaches (see Hugman and Smith, 1995). It was argued that the Kantian approach, especially that element that proposed the humanity of each individual as an end as well as a means and recognised each actual person as an instance of the general, established ethics as impersonal principles and removed them from the world of social relations. The individualisation that Biestek claimed as central to social work ethics and which emphasised the status of the client as a unique person was criticised by Marxists, for example, for taking the individual out of the context of the social relations in which he/she is located.

Feminists and anti-racist critiques developed in the late 1970s and 1980s were critical of preceding Marxist approaches because of the primacy attached to class, thus ignoring gendered and racialised forms of oppression. These critiques found expression in the Requirements for the Diploma in Social Work (CCETSW, 1991). These urged qualifying workers to develop an awareness of structural oppression, to understand and counteract stigma and discrimination at both an institutional and individual level, and to develop policies and practices that were non-discriminatory and anti-oppressive. At the time, Jordan (1991) argued that running alongside what could be called the radical/structural parts of the regulations were more traditional injunctions including a client's rights to dignity, privacy, confidentiality and choice. This latter list had its roots in liberal ethics, market minded politics, casework and law and there was thus a tension between the different sets of values which was not adequately acknowledged or explored.

These regulations were to achieve a level of contention and to be subject to sustained criticism (see Denney 1996)[1] and were revised. However, a key point is that in the subsequent decades there was an emphasis, especially in the kinds of texts influential in social work education on oppression, that led to a rigid prescriptive approach that often obscured the kinds of troubling questions that are raised when one has a universal approach to respecting all human beings as Featherstone and Lancaster (1997) argued in their analysis of policy and practice towards men who sexually abuse. They argued there had been a shift away from respect for persons and non-judgmentalism to anti-oppressive and anti-discriminatory approaches which had not received adequate scrutiny ethically and were not informed by thoughtful theoretical frameworks. They therefore ran the risk of reinforcing the divisive and harsh social policies of the time.

Indeed, the emergence and entrenchment of an audit culture in those decades was to reinforce moves towards a hierarchy of who was entitled to respect, to be heard and to be treated as means and ends. In a very important chapter, which is still pertinent today, Howe (1996) argued that the apparent failure of the welfare state to guarantee safety, personal growth and improved behaviour, alongside its alleged undermining of initiative, independence and creativity had seen a swing in the 1980s and 1990s to a radical re-emphasis on human freedom. He noted that social work had undergone a number of changes accordingly. He considered these to encompass three areas: the performance of clients; competencies and the performance of social workers; and social work in the market place. In terms of clients, there had been a switch from exploring the causes of why behaviour emerged to addressing their performance and how it could be monitored and audited. In Chapter Seven where we look at men who are violent we will explore how this has played out in practice.

In the mid-1990s a number of books emerged explicitly devoted to looking at ethics and values in social work and probation work (Banks, 1995; Hugman and Smith, 1995; Williams, 1995). Such books reflected wider trends in an interdisciplinary scholarship drawing on postmodern and feminist literatures. Hugman and Smith argued for recognising ethical issues as inevitably specific and contextualised. While this recognition clearly owed a strong debt to writers within the ethic of care, this debt was not always acknowledged (Orme, 2001, 2002).

The origins of the ethics of care lie in the work of Carol Gilligan (for an overview see Featherstone and Morris, 2012). Her book *In a Different Voice* (1983) opened up discussions in moral theory, feminism, and theories of the subject. She challenged the then influential approach of Kohlberg, her teacher, a Harvard psychologist, whose work was underpinned by Kant's understandings whose studies had concluded women stayed at an inferior stage of moral development with few attaining the highest stages of moral reasoning. She argued, however, that men in considering ethical dilemmas operated within a frame which considered abstract notions of right or wrong whereas women operated within a context that considered specific relationships and responsibilities. She named these as an ethic of justice that stressed rights and rules and an ethic of care that was tied to concrete circumstances and activities rather than philosophical abstractions. Her work was controversial and influential. She was considered essentialist and anti-feminist: the work seemed to promote women as morally superior to men, thus inverting Kolberg and also posed a binary that was considered very unhelpful – between justice and care. Subsequent work has tried to resolve this latter issue. For Tronto (1993, 2010), for example, care should not be counterposed to justice, but seen as a set of activities and a social process engendering important aspects of citizenship. The process of caring for – or being cared for – makes one aware of diversity, interdependence, and the need to accept difference. This awareness provides an important basis for citizenship and is as likely, or more likely, to be learned through care as through paid work practices.

Hekman (1995) has argued Gilligan's work was both an indication of, and a major contributor to, a sea change underway in late 20th century intellectual thought. There was an already existing move away from the universalism and absolutism of modernist epistemology towards conceptions emphasising particularity and concreteness. The linchpin was the attack on the centrepiece of moral philosophy and modernist Enlightenment epistemology: man as the rational, abstract autonomous constitutor of knowledge. Gilligan identified the ethical code of Western societies as based upon universalisable concepts, such as objectivity and partiality, which reflected a partial and masculine worldview. Although not a moral philosopher, Hekman argued that Gilligan had made a major contribution to moral philosophy.

In an application to social work, Orme (2002) has argued that contributions within the ethics of care literature and, in particular, debates about the relationship between care and justice opened up important possibilities, outlining the need for a dialogical approach to justice:

> A dialogical approach to justice challenges the binaries not only of care/justice but also those of private/public, carer/cared for ... such an interplay allows for perspectives other than gender to inform and complicate ethical choice ... traditional ethics heard a single voice of disembodied moral principles, *feminist ethics listens to and hears multiple voices because it defines morality and moral knowledge as plural and heterogeneous.* This plurality is vital within community care because social work needs to challenge the excessive bureaucratization of confining those who require care, and indeed those who provide it, into constrained homogenized categories of, for example, older people, people with

disabilities or those with mental health problems.(Orme, 2002: 809, emphasis added)

In more recent years, there has been an influential contribution from those concerned with Aristotelian virtue ethics. Webb (2006) argues, in a context where a preoccupation with knowing and eliminating risk has hollowed out the social work project, the moral identity of the social worker needs to be recast in terms of virtue ethics. Classically juxtaposed and contrasted with Plato's Utopian engineering, which is characterised by a rigid attachment to a blueprint for changing society, virtue ethics suggests that what we need instead is something much more dialogical. The right answers must be negotiated in context, with attention to the particulars of this family in this situation, not an appeal to what are inevitably fictitious universals held in place by expert discourses (MacIntyre, 1997) – technical fixes in other words!

Virtue ethics is a normative theory emphasising a person's character and the way they reach judgements. It is usually seen as running counter to rule-bound or duty-bound conceptions of moral principles and as we have noted above the hierarchical basis of Plato's world view (Plato, 2007). Derived from the classical writings of Aristotle, virtues are admirable human dispositions that can be learned and distinguish good people from bad (Webb, 2006: 22). Thus the basic question to be asked is not just what constitutes good social work, but rather what is a good social worker?

> Virtue ethics emphasises the priority of the moral agent who has acquired virtues commensurate with the pursuit of a revisable conception of the good life – the *well-fare* of all in a defined community. The virtues are the acquired inner qualities of humans –character – the possession of which, if applied in due measure, will typically contribute to the realisation of the good life. ... Virtue ethics is especially distinct from its rivals by pointing the ethical way back to the need for the cultivation of character, and thus to the precedence of the quality of the actor over that of the action. (Webb, 2006: 219)

Doing the right thing in social work is not a matter of applying moral concepts or rules, nor is it an implicit aspect of the work or activity in which the social worker engages. Doing the right thing comes from the social worker as agent practising the virtues. These are generalisable capacities of self, the application of which is acquired through training and experience and crucially they always involve choice and judgement. The famous doctrine of the Golden Mean is not a mathematical notion, but one dependent on judgement about the best point between two extremes. It is neither too little nor too much and because these are judgements there can be no universal rule, except that there is no universal rule!

Central to the move away from notions of the individual deciding in isolation upon what is the right thing to do has been the rethinking of how we come to be 'understood', indeed recognised, and the inter-subjective processes that contribute. The notion of recognition has emerged in the last few decades from diverse fields with substantial contributions from a range of thinkers as well as considerable debate and disagreement. Philosophical interest dates back to Hegel who first coined the term 'struggle for recognition' (McQueen, 2011). He was countering Descartes' dualistic philosophy in which the mind was seen as a private theatre and knowledge of the self was achieved through introspection. Hegel argued self-knowledge, one's sense of freedom and sense of self were not a matter of introspection but required the recognition of another. He developed this further in later work where it became an essential factor in the development of ethical life. The master–slave dialect has been enormously influential in terms of understanding 'the struggle for recognition'. The master has power over the slave, reducing him/her to the status of thing. While the slave receives no recognition from the master, the master requires the recognition of the slave, although it is worthless as it is not the recognition of a free consciousness. Only free consciousness can grant the recognition required for self-certainty of existence and freedom. Indeed, relations of domination provide a vicious spiral of recognition. Recognition must always take place between equals, mediated through social institutions that can guarantee that equality and produce the necessary mutual relations of recognition necessary for the attainment of freedom.

There are a number of highly influential contemporary theorists of recognition (for example, Axel Honneth and Nancy Fraser). Honneth (1995) defines recognition as follows:

> (H)uman individuation is a process in which the individual can unfold a practical identity to the extent that he is capable of reassuring himself of recognition by a growing circle of partners to communication. Subjects ... are constituted as individuals solely by learning, from the perspective of

others who offer approval, to relate to themselves as beings
who possess certain positive qualities and abilities. (p 189)

Honneth identifies three spheres of interaction which are connected
to three patterns of recognition that are necessary for an individual
to develop a positive self: love, rights and solidarity. Love refers to our
physical needs and emotions being met. Rights refer to social and
legal exclusion, and solidarity relates to recognition of our individual
abilities (esteem). Honneth argues material inequality is a facet of a
more profound disrespect, indeed a lack of recognition which has its
origins in early infant–mother dynamics.

Nancy Fraser's work has been concerned to reconcile recognition
with redistribution noting a division between those seeking more
equal distribution of resources and those groups seeking recognition
of their 'difference'. She seeks to reconcile these using an expanded
concept of justice (see, for example, Fraser, 1997, 2000). For Fraser,
lack of recognition springs from damaging cultural representation of
particular groups, such as women, whereas lack of material resources
springs from power inequalities in relation to the distribution of
resources (see Fowler, 2009, for a discussion).

While both Honneth and Fraser aim to ground the normative
political implications of their work in a critical analysis of contemporary
power relations, there is a basic disagreement between them about
how to characterise the dynamics of contemporary social and political
conflict:

> For Honneth, all such conflicts, including those over
> economic distribution, are variants of a fundamental struggle
> for recognition that itself is the key to understanding the
> long-term development of social interaction in capitalist
> societies. Against this, Fraser argues that struggles for
> recognition, such as identity politics, are analytically distinct
> from conflicts over redistribution. Both are fundamental
> to social justice but are irreducible to each other. (McNay,
> 2008: 271)

Butler takes a more radically deconstructive approach than either. While
recognising the importance of the Hegelian tradition, she suggests that
a number of important points are missed:

> The terms by which we are recognised as human are socially
> articulated and changeable. And sometimes the very terms

that confer 'humanness' on some individuals are those that deprive certain other individuals of the possibility of achieving that status, producing a differential between the human and the less–than–human. (Butler, 2004: 2)

In recent work she has drawn explicitly from the work of Levinas. His lifelong work on ethics was a response to the catastrophic failure of ethics enacted in the Holocaust. He was a student of Heidegger whose turn to Nazism probably inspired his core preoccupation: what is the problem with knowledge and philosophy if Heidegger failed to grasp the evil of Nazism? He answers this by insisting on the primacy of ethics before knowledge and philosophy (see Rossiter, 2011, for an interesting review and application to social work). At the heart of his ethics is the notion that our representations of persons are always inadequate – something always overflows, escapes our knowledge, comprehension, conceptions. Levinas wants us to greet the other with the conviction that the other person can never be fully known through our representation of him/her. A key concept for Levinas is what he calls 'the face' – the face represents the demand for response that is initiated in the face's approach to another person. The face appears from a height, destitute and requiring response from the other. The face is both a supplicant and a commander: it both needs us and demands our response. For Levinas the presence of the face and its demand for response are the start of ethics itself – the presence of the face initiates ethics because we are not free to not respond, even if this response is turning away.

Drawing from the work of Levinas, Butler (2005: 91) argues that we need to affirm the unfreedom at the heart of our relations with each other:

> I cannot disavow my relation to the Other regardless of what the Other does, regardless of what I might will. Indeed, responsibility is not a matter of cultivating a will, but of making use of an unwilled susceptibility as a resource for becoming responsive to the Other. Whatever the Other has done, the Other still makes an ethical demand upon me, has a 'face' to which I am obliged to respond – meaning that I am, as it were, precluded from revenge by virtue of a relation I never chose. (Butler, 2005: 91)

Butler, in obliging us to embrace the stranger, draws attention to inclusion and exclusion in the very notion of who is considered human.

While this has clear implications in her earlier analyses for engaging with how the norms that structure intelligible gendered 'positions' and sexualities work, she has extended the conversation in her later work to consider who is able to be heard, whose lives can be grieved for and so on, as she has taken on very public roles as a critic of US and Israeli foreign policy in particular. Butler opens up possibilities for rigorous painful conversations. Who can be heard, whose suffering can be grieved for? Who is left out in the narratives that predominate? She obliges us to think again about all those we work with, not just to pick out a legitimate 'victim'. She has also argued that if society prevents us from thinking about what we ought to think about, the experience is foreclosed because there is no public recognition or discourse through which it might be named and mourned. Thus birth parents who lose their children to the child protection system are often completely disenfranchised in this way and it is scarcely surprising that many go on to have successive children removed. Indeed, Nick Crichton (2012), a district judge in London who set up the pioneering drug and alcohol treatment court there, notes that his impetus was the numbers of birth parents having successive children removed, in the absence of focused and purposeful help for their substance misuse and relationship difficulties.

Thinking ethically about working with those who harm themselves and others

> The tragedy is that none of us automatically responds to hardship, humiliation or the abusive exercise of power through noble resistance, we are just as likely to turn our sense of grievance upon ourselves or innocent others. This is suffering turned upon itself and it is this double suffering which is often the subject of professional practice in welfare work. (Frost and Hoggett, 2008: 455)

Frost and Hoggett have developed an important analysis of responses to social suffering using the concept of 'double suffering'. As we explored in the last chapter, the notion of social suffering as developed by Bourdieu (1999) emphasises not just the unequal distribution of material goods in society but also people's lived experiences of oppression and the feelings of humiliation, anger, resentment, despair that can accompany oppression: 'using material poverty as the sole measure of all suffering keeps us from seeing and understanding a whole side of the suffering characteristic of the social order' (Bourdieu, 1999: 4).

Frost and Hoggett argue that some experiences threaten to go beyond our capacity to digest them because we lack the resources to symbolise and give meaning to them. They are more likely to be experiences that have been forced upon us rather than ones we have freely chosen, those we face as powerless objects rather than as active agents. If experience cannot be thought about then we will have an unreflexive relation to it. If suffering cannot be thought about, it will be somatised and embodied, acted out or projected.

In terms of somatised or embodied practices, social suffering is inscribed on the body: the low self-esteem, low status, lack of social capital and lack of power to direct one's own life are written on the body and manifest in health inequalities and also self-destructive behaviours. Suffering is enacted through behaviour that is damaging or harmful to places (for example, anti-social behaviour). Suffering can also be projected onto others including most obviously those more vulnerable:

> Subjects of social suffering may not draw easily upon our compassion if they do not present themselves as innocent victims, but as aggressive, resentful or suspicious people whose hurt and loss is directed at others rather than at themselves. (Frost and Hoggett: 453)

Frost and Hoggett name the ethical challenges especially when we encounter those who are profoundly marginalised who are harming others and it is of course the difficulties here that can lead to the taking of seductive short cuts: 'I'm only here for the child!'

But this seductive short cut can become a cul-de-sac with longstanding consequences. It is sobering to reflect on the research evidence that suggests current practices with *all* members within families are riven by exclusions and lack of communication. Indeed concrete initiatives have emerged to counter such processes such as Family Group Conferences and there is some evidence to suggest they can offer a way of ensuring multiple voices can be heard and possibilities for dialogue in 'protected' spaces.

But these conferences are not in the mainstream and we note our findings from evaluations of independent advocacy services for parents and family and friends carers that spaces for multiple voices and uncoerced speech remain fragile (Featherstone et al, 2011; Featherstone and Fraser, 2012a).

Family Rights Group (FRG)[2] provides a professional advocacy service which targets parents whose children are particularly at risk of suffering significant harm, and being removed from their parental home. Direct face-to-face advocacy is provided from the point of initial investigation to the first child protection review conference. Indirect Advocacy is the practice of professional advocates negotiating by letter, email or telephone on the service user's behalf, or with the service user on an ongoing basis in the name of FRG. The advocacy projects developed by the Family Rights Group draw upon the evidence of a qualitative research study on specialist advice and advocacy for parents in child protection cases (1997–2001) and are informed by the associated protocol funded by the Department of Health (Lindley and Richards, 2002). The authors drew on relevant policy and research literature to inform this work.

A brief summary of key themes from the protocol developed by Lindley and Richards is offered here:

- It is crucial that advocates are independent of all agencies involved in child protection work. However, independence needs to be worked at rather than assumed and vigilance is required to ensure it is not jeopardised.
- Advocates need to be clear that while it is not their responsibility to undertake the making of enquiries where there is a suspicion of harm to children, it is essential that they do not conceal information about any continuing or likely harm to a child. While the advocate is not under a statutory duty to report information about such harm to the local authority, advocates with a professional qualification (for example, solicitors or social workers) are under a professional duty to do so and others are under a moral duty to do so.
- Training and supervision arrangements should be developed by those offering advocacy services in order to support the making of judgements by advocates about harm thresholds.
- The intervention by the advocate is on behalf of parents and not undertaken by the advocate in their own right.
- The advocate must decline to give their opinion about risk or registration or the plans being put forward even if invited to.
- The advocate should not withhold information from the parent.
- Advocates are there for parents and are therefore partisan but should be supported to remain dispassionate.

Advocates operate within an ethic of care; they offer rights based advice in a context of stressing the importance of working within relationships, whatever the individuals may have done, or are suspected of having done. This is complex work in a context where there are multiple stakeholders. The evaluations have highlighted the possibilities they offer to service users to exercise voice and experience being heard in very daunting circumstances such as, for example, the case conference process:

> 'The meeting went on for five hours and he [father of children] was making himself look good and calling me a liar and I just sat there and I thought I can't be bothered. I haven't got time for talking, I've got three children to look after ... I just felt the pressure, I've got a special needs child who's got learning difficulties and I couldn't cope, he's just too much, I'm a human at the end of the day and I've got feelings but I just had them all there [conference professionals] and it's like everybody took power and I didn't have any say ... I just lost confidence in everybody, I lost trust completely.' (Sumetra, a mother)

Sunetra's experience chimes with that of others on the impact of the child protection conference. Indeed some professionals are clear on this too:

> 'I mean they're very daunting things, conferences, and although you know, as chair I, and I'm sure my colleagues, you do your best to support and encourage a parent to speak and whatever, you know, it's not an easy place to be.' (Conference chairperson)

There are clearly pressing challenges in creating conversations in the context of maltreatment of children. It requires a complex and nuanced understanding of humanity and suffering and an acknowledgement that malign actions often take place as emotional responses are refracted through the prisms of shame, rage or passive desperation. Understanding the emotional lives of parents does not excuse cruelty, does not do away with the need for punishment and societal retribution, does not mean children should be left in danger to prevent further harm to parents, but it does create the possibility for conversations and thus for change. To achieve this, social workers need to have sophisticated vocabularies and a mistrust of claims to have found final (technical and linguistic) settlements. Arguing for the vitality (in both senses) of agile vocabularies, Lewis Hyde notes:

> We may well hope our actions carry no moral ambiguity, but pretending that is the case when it isn't doesn't lead to

greater clarity about right and wrong; it more likely leads to unconscious cruelty masked by inflated righteousness. (Hyde 1998: 11)

Concluding remarks

We concur with Lonne et al on the parameters of what an ethically articulate project should encompass:

> ... to consider and balance different principles, respect the rights of multiple stakeholders, understand the demands of the specific context, face the uncertainty of judgements about immediate and longer-term outcomes, and ... the challenge to become professionals of integrity who not only do the right thing but are the sort of people who do the right thing. (Lonne et al, 2009: 129)

Houston (2010) has argued that although different schools of ethics have been hard to reconcile they need to be in a world where social workers have to engage with legal injunctions, procedural rules, the future consequences of decision making, issues that have a bearing on professional integrity and situations of care. Thus deontology (rules) and consequentialism (consequences of one's actions) need to be integrated into understandings of care (ethics of care) and professional integrity and careful contingent judgements (virtue ethics). Houston argues for a form of discourse ethics to underpin this project as for him communication and inter-subjective engagement are the only media through which actors can reach morally binding decisions. This is echoed by Amartya Sen who argues 'the status that ... ethical claims have must be ultimately dependent on their survivability in unobstructed discussion' (2005: 160). Similarly, Bernstein (1983) argues for a:

> ... defence of the Socratic virtues, "the willingness to talk, to listen to other people, to weigh the consequences of our actions upon other people" ... It means turning away from the obsession "to get things right" and turning our attention to coping with the contingencies of human life. (Bernstein, 1983: 203)

For Bernstein, it is a *moral* imperative to defend 'the openness of human conversation against all those temptations and real threats that seek closure' (1983: 204–5). Such a vision acknowledges the inevitability of conflicting perspectives, and it also highlights the dangers of monopoly positions on truth, which limit debate.

We have argued here that broader debates need to occur about the purpose of interventions – this is not just an issue for social workers and service users but involves much wider forces and considerations including the fostering of engagement with civil society as the means by which families can flourish safely, with respect and sometimes with vital moral opprobrium from each other.

Notes

[1] Media attention focused on an adoption case involving a 'mixed race' child in Norfolk amid debate over the practice of ethnic matching.

[2] Family Rights Group is a charity that operates in England and Wales offering support to parents and family and friends carers so that children may be enabled to be cared for safely within their networks.

FOUR

Developing research mindedness in learning cultures

> This review recommends a radical reduction in the amount of central prescription to help professionals move from *a compliance culture to a learning culture*, where they have more freedom to use their *expertise* in assessing need and providing the right help. (Munro, 2011: 6–7, emphasis added)

In the quotation above, Eileen Munro recommends a shift in professional cultures, so expertise is valued and organisational learning flourishes. We share these aspirations, but attempting to achieve them in the current context of child and family social work is likely to produce some vexing challenges. 'Expertise' is hydra headed, and each of its heads – research, evidence, intuition, practice wisdom – is two-faced. All are malleable and may be used both to open up and to delimit debate. Claims to expertise are often politicised and readily conscripted into moral missions. A learning culture should foster a rigorous scepticism about grand claims. The problems with which social work engages are ancient and recalcitrant. Only the most nuanced arguments hold any real promise, yet these are often conspicuous by their absence. Rather truth claims are made and abundance is duly conquered (Feyerabend, 2001): only a narrow range of sanctioned 'disposals' survives the bigotry of the policy process. It seems we can see complexity and nuance in our own lives but not in lives of the children and families who come to the attention of our social work services. 'We' need help, 'they' need intervention.

In this book, we make a case for family-minded, humane social work practice. Clearly, ethical engagement with the professional task involves two primary imperatives: first, borrowing from the Hippocratic Oath, 'do no harm', and second 'do some good'. These have been joined increasingly by a third 'show you have done some good' and a fourth 'show how much it costs'. These requirements depend on the examination and interrogation of professional activities and their effects. They depend upon research. Used in this way, research can help to protect families from harmful or useless interventions, focus professional time on the most efficacious practices and services, and ensure value for money in stricken times. Moreover, research can open to scrutiny and debate routine institutional practices and taken for granted ways of operating, thus nurturing a learning culture. Research is a good thing.

Yet research itself, or rather our ideas about it and how it should properly be conducted, constitute sites of contestation and struggle with very high stakes. Research and what counts as valid knowledge are political matters. We will argue here that social work has a particular capacity to colonise and be colonised by shifting sets of received ideas, often highly normative in nature, into which various research findings and theoretical constructs are recruited. Both evidence-based practice and evidence-based policy presuppose that if we address vexing questions with appropriate rigour, technical solutions will become available. But, as we shall see in due course, applying a technical solution to moral or ethical problems is not without consequence. The purpose of this chapter is not to review the range and types of social work research, nor to rehearse in detail the debates about the relative merits of particular methods (for a comprehensive and informed source on these matters, see Shaw et al, 2009); rather we want to explore the politics of contemporary debates about evidence and practice and how these relate to the dominant models of service delivery we are challenging in this book. For the practitioners and managers among our readers, we want to stress the importance and vitality of research in the production of organisational learning. Many data are routinely gathered in contemporary organisations and are usually under-analysed both within the organisations themselves, and within the government departments demanding that they are gathered (Broadhurst et al, 2009). Data can show unexpected patterns, raise new questions and stimulate debate. It is also vital that organisations take steps to examine systematically the impact of their interventions on families. Families' and children's stories matter. Research, then, is everybody's business. However, and crucially, we also want to urge that not too much is taken on trust. A great many interventions and ambitious policy initiatives claim to be evidence-based. These claims usually have some validity but the nature of the evidence, the way it was produced and its context are crucial, and often unacknowledged in the reforming zeal of the policy process. Expertise and evidence are related but they are not the same thing. One must be made to interrogate the other and we must examine the conditions under which some ideas flourish while others are snuffed out.

The movement of thought and the development of scientific understandings are social in nature and knowledge does necessarily reliably proceed on a 'survival of the fittest' basis. In any domain, new understandings, and indeed forgotten ones, are not evaluated dispassionately for their intrinsic value, rather they run like raindrops down a pane, sticky with current orthodoxies, and many do not make it into practice, or do so only slowly and circuitously. This is so, even in more technological domains like medicine and pharmacology: for example, the hypothesis generated during the mid–1980s that gastric ulcers were the result of infection with a bacterium *Helicobacter Pylori* was initially considered preposterous. Despite the rigour of the experiments, the established belief that peptic ulcers were caused by excess acidity which eventually eroded the stomach wall meant the new hypothesis was resisted by both scientists and clinicians. It was over a decade before the idea gained widespread acceptance (Thagard, 2000). So, there is a good deal more to evidence than getting the experiments right. If this is so in biomedicine, it is amplified in social work, with its intrinsically normative agendas. The public and its populist tribunes are often raucous and opinionated about social work and politicians are thus incited to act with alacrity to fix the 'problem family' once and for all!

We argue here that research and how it is made and used in organisations, policy and practice demand investigation in their own right. The concept of a learning organisation is predicated on the ability to see what Argyris (1999) calls 'defensive routines', which sustain established patterns and are usually taken for granted and difficult to spot.

> Teams stay stuck in their defensive routines only when they pretend that they don't have any defensive routines, that everything is all right, and that they can say 'anything'. But how to make them discussable is a challenge. (Senge, 1990: 255)

Social work has its defensive routines and it forgets its own histories. If our agencies are to become learning organisations, we are going to have to develop ways to make these visible. Research can help us to do this but methods wars, misreadings, selective interpretations and overblown claims about 'evidence' can help hold defensive routines in place with profound consequences for children and families, and indeed for social work organisations. We begin this chapter with an examination of the ideologies of practice and the misappropriation of 'evidence' in their support; we move on to consider the politics of evidence, examining how some ideas flourish whilst others gasp for air. We conclude with some recommendations for the development of organisational cultures where curiosity and debate can thrive.

Misuses and misreadings: research, policy and practice as social drama

> When five-year old Jehan Martin was murdered in 1457, the culprits were quickly apprehended, imprisoned and brought to trial. The case followed the normal procedure for such a crime, except in one important respect, the accused were pigs. ... The judgement that followed was unusually tricky, since one of the animals appeared more culpable than the others. The child was killed by a sow in the presence of six piglets. These were stained with blood ... but there was no 'positive proof that they had assisted in mangling the deceased'. After consulting with local experts, the judge ruled that the sow should be executed. (Oldridge, 2007: 40)

Trials of animals were common in the pre-modern age, conducted with the full ceremony of law and with due attendance to evidence and legal representation for the accused. They were completely rational within the belief system of that time. That is the problem with belief systems: they govern beliefs, which seem, in turn, to be the only right and proper ways to think. When we examine the history of child care social work in the UK, there are numerous examples of particular orthodoxies taking hold. The fickle pendulum has swung on transracial adoption, family support or child protection, planning for permanency for children in care. Dominant forms of practice are often only visible when they are breached, or when they over-reach themselves. During the late 1980s, 'anatomically correct' dolls were routinely used by local authority social workers to interview suspected victims of child sexual abuse. The Cleveland Inquiry in 1987 (Butler-Sloss, 1988) signalled the end of that particular orthodoxy as social workers were criticised for 'overzealous' intrusion into family life (Parton, 1991), based, as it happens, on example of misguided empirics and faulty attribution of causation known as 'reflex anal dilatation' (the alleged and now discredited 'finding' that the anuses of children who had been anally abused dilated in response to examination and therefore reflex anal dilatation was a *diagnostic* sign of abuse). We can say from our own experience that 'disclosure interviews' felt alright at the time, but clearly they were deeply problematic.

Fashionable and powerful ideas, often supported by theory, selective readings and misreading of evidence or varieties of moral reasoning, can interrupt the capacity of practitioners to engage critically with their endeavour. When making their case for this or that course of action practitioners may be unaware that they are invoking an 'idea', and that this idea exists among many alternatives which may have become obscured by the current settlement. Professionals may be free and purposeful agents, but not in conditions of their own making. For example, there was a time quite recently when there was no concept of a 'disorganised attachment' (see Shemmings and Shemmings, 2011, for a review). There may have been a set of observed behaviours, but they had not been glossed into a category and there was not a research programme dedicated to fluffing and filling out the category. To create that category a great deal of improvisation in laboratories had to take place. For example in their 1992 paper, Van Ijzendoorn et al note:

> Although disorganized attachment behavior is necessarily difficult to observe and often subtle, many researchers have managed to become reliable coders. … In normal, middle class families, about 15% of the infants develop disorganized attachment behavior. In other social contexts and in clinical groups this percentage may become twice or even three times higher (e.g., in the case of maltreatment). Although the importance of disorganized attachment for developmental psychopathology is evident, the search for the mechanisms leading to disorganization has just started. (1992: 225)

In the paper's discussion section it is noted that, for diagnostic purposes, the coding system for disorganised attachment is very complicated and the intercoder reliability only marginal – different observers see different patterns in other words. A noteworthy example cited is a case in which the 'detection' of disorganised attachment in a child's home took, 'almost 4 hr of videotaped observations, with a further frustration that the attachment figure did not always show the behaviour that triggered a disorganized response of the infant' (p 249). The authors of the meta-analysis urge a search for 'ethically acceptable ways of inducing these triggering behaviours in the parent' (Van Ijzendoorn et al, 1992: 242). This is a somewhat troubling idea in itself, and a clear marker of the incertitude of the knowledge reviewed. Calling for further research, the paper concludes:

> we should be cautious … about the diagnostic use of disorganized attachment … the meta-analytic evidence presented in this paper is only correlational and the causal nature of the association between disorganized

attachment and externalizing problem behavior still has to be established. (1992: 244)

Some years on and the artfulness of the construction of the category and the capacity for observation to be over-determined by theory is entirely forgotten. Of course, this does not make the category useless, but neither does it make it infallible!

A learning culture needs to promote the interrogation of such categories and of their effects, not so that they may be abandoned – although some may be – but so that they can be critically appraised. As we shall show shortly, the current settlement in child welfare is marked by a doctrine of 'child-centredness' with powerful a priori correctness and a fierce moral force into which 'evidence' is selectively conscripted. If that statement makes you feel uncomfortable, then we rest our case.

Greenhalgh and Russell note:

> ... "evidence" for policy making is not sitting in journals ready to be harvested. ... Rather, it is dynamically created through the human interaction around the policy making table – and, probably more significantly, the lobbying, campaigning and interpersonal influencing going on in the back rooms and corridors leading up to official policy making meetings. (2006: 36–7)

This statement has particular veracity in the domain of family policy. The policies of right wing governments are notoriously unfriendly to the poor, but attempts by governments of every hue to influence parenting have a long and not altogether pretty history. In 1896 the socialist Sidney Webb urged the Fabians to 'take property from idle rich and children from the unfit poor' (Chesterton and Perry, 2000: 7). The right want to cleanse, the left want to save the children. Victorian reformers made their case using evidence from new science of eugenics. Discredited by the Nazis eugenics by that name has (for now) had its day, but the moral mission remains intact and its capacity to support itself with science is unimpeded by modern sensibilities. Commenting on the unprecedented increase in the numbers of care proceedings in the UK on BBC Radio 4's *Today* programme (9 February 2012), the President of the Association of Directors of Children's Services observed that this was due to

> 'a better understanding of the corrosive and damaging impact of neglect on children's development ... it is about

understanding the effect of neglectful parenting due to drug and alcohol problems and the physical damage to brain development it can do with very young children.'

This version of eugenics without the genes is elucidated at length in a report on early intervention by the MP Graham Allen (Allen 2011a and b) commissioned by the UK government. The neuroscience of the infant brain figures prominently; the brain is mentioned 59 times, and the cover carries dramatic images of an infant brain damaged by neglect. However, as Greenhalgh and Russell note above, this is evidence dynamically created on the social stage. A careful reading of the research cited (Wastell and White, 2012) reveals that it does not support the strong assertion that children's brains are uniquely vulnerable to lasting damage by the sorts of neglect routinely encountered in UK services. We are not told the origin of either of the brains on the front cover, but drilling down into the literature one finds that the brain on the right belongs to a Romanian orphan suffering extreme institutional neglect and about whose history and pre-morbidities we know nothing.

The preoccupation with neuroscience is further evidenced in another government commissioned report, this time explicitly termed an 'evidence review' with a primary purposes of 'training' child welfare professionals and the family judiciary in child development. In the document *Decision-making within the child's time frame* (Brown and Ward, 2013), the authors state that the evidence in the main body of the report is drawn 'from papers which reported on, or which provided a methodologically sound review of primary research' (p 9), complemented by recent government funded reports and material which can be 'easily accessed by family justice professionals', such as the Center for the Developing Child at Harvard University.

These inclusion and exclusion decisions seem to have had an effect on the neuroscientific strand of the work. In essence, the report appears to present current debates within the field as reflecting consensually agreed, certain knowledge that children's brains are readily susceptible to irreversible damage by less than optimal parenting. That the neuroscientific claims in recent policy have been met with such credulity by many merits examination. The purpose of the Harvard Center is to synthesise and make accessible neuroscientific findings, as one of its founders explains:

> Science has an important role to play in advising policymakers on crafting effective responses to social problems that affect the development of children. This article describes lessons

learned from a multiyear, working collaboration among
neuroscientists, developmental psychologists, pediatricians,
economists, and communications researchers who are
engaged in the iterative construction of a core story of
development, using simplifying models (i.e., metaphors)
such as 'brain architecture,' 'toxic stress,' and 'serve and return'
to explain complex scientific concepts to non-scientists.
(Shonkoff and Bales, 2011: 17)

Well intentioned and helpful though such syntheses can be, in their
desire to persuade, they gloss complexity. It is important to read the
original research, which usually gives a much more realistic account of
the fragilities of the knowledge base. It is very much more optimistic
about the resilience of the infant brain and cautious about the dangers
of extrapolating from studies of extreme clinical populations like the
Romanian orphans and from animal studies. The science is not yet
clear, or policy ready, as is evidenced in two recent authoritative reviews
(Belsky and de Haan, 2011; McCrory et al, 2012), and thus must be
treated with caution when applied to policy and practice contexts. The
helping professions, as Gambrill (2012) notes, are particularly susceptible
to what she calls 'propaganda' in the modern age:

It is time to pay more attention to propaganda in the
helping professions... Are your beliefs engineered by
others based on bogus grounds promoted by staff in public
relations agencies... That is, has an illusion of knowledge
(or ignorance) been created? Are your beliefs about the
prevalence and causes of normal variations in behaviour
influenced by psychiatrists on the payroll of pharmaceutical
companies serving as 'opinion leaders'? Are these beliefs
accurate? Does it make any difference as long as you 'feel
free' – as long as you believe that you made an informed
choice...? (25)

At this point we need to attend to the politics of evidence in social
work and consider its consequences.

Research and learning: the politics of evidence

... methodology, whilst masquerading as the epitome
of rationality, has the potential to operate as a ritual,
whose enactment provides individuals with a feeling of

effectiveness but which in reality alienates them from their real task. (Wastell, 1996: 38)

In this extract, we are warned about the fetish of methods, where particular ways of capturing and interpreting data about the world become privileged. When this happens in child welfare, as we shall see, it has the capacity artificially to delimit the range of sanctioned and funded practices, resources and interventions. Social work is an applied social science and it is pleasing to note that, within its journals and learned texts, there are reasoned debates, methodological pluralism and innovation and productive, occasionally even wise, questioning of what counts as a fact. 'Journal science' in social work as in other domains is often tentative, provisional and dialogical. But, something happens to this tentative knowledge as it passes into textbooks and handbooks and ultimately onto posters and into pamphlets replete with research sound bites. It loses its provisional quality. The philosopher of science Ludwik Fleck, writing originally in the 1930s, calls this 'vade-mecum' knowledge. Translated from the Latin this means 'go with me': vade-mecum knowledge is knowledge 'to go'. Handbook knowledge is not simply a distillation of journal science, which is often characterised by contradictory claims. Rather the vade-mecum selects and assembles artefacts from journal science. Once assembled, this new, more certain science appears axiomatic and thereby has the potential to constrain thinking. Fleck notes:

> If a fact is taken to mean something fixed and proven, it exists only in vade-mecum science. The preliminary stage of disjointed signals of resistance within journal science really constitutes only the predisposition for a fact. Later, at the stage of popular knowledge, the fact becomes incarnated as an ... object of reality. (Fleck, 1979: 124–5)

As handbook science travels yet further away from its sites of production via the media into the popular domain its status becomes even more simplified and 'certain'. Popular science is characterised by the omission of detail and crucially of dissenting or controversial opinion. It is this knowledge that so appeals to policy makers, but it is only when science has travelled far from its sites of production that it is amenable to the simplification necessary for incorporation into protocols and guidelines. At this point caution is needed in its interpretation. Yet protocols, guidelines and colourful flow charts are the very stuff of organisational life. They seem to offer the promise of tried and tested knowledge, but they have not arrived on your desk by a process of natural selection.

Currently in child and family social work we are seeing a troubling resolution of the process of translation of research into policy and practice, which threatens to derail Munro's project to make organisational learning and humane practice a reality. In the policy domain, we witness the privileging of a particular method for evaluating interventions, the randomised controlled trial (RCT), the high watermark of evidence-based medicine. Evidence-based medicine has a clear hierarchy of evidence, with RCTs at the top providing 'gold standard' against which all else can be judged. RCTs randomly allocate patients between a group who will receive the treatment under investigation and a control group who will receive a placebo (or no treatment) and/or an existing conventional treatment, ideally neither the clinician nor the patient should know who is receiving the treatment (that is, the trial should be 'double blind'). Meta-analyses and systematic reviews of RCTs are at the very pinnacle of the hierarchy of evidence. A range of specialist centres such as the Cochrane Centre in Oxford, (named after Professor A.L. Cochrane who, during the early 1970s, argued for and eventually popularised the randomised controlled trial) have been established to scrutinise research findings for evidence of bias or other flaws in design.

In social work, RCTs are rather more challenging to apply, but they have a number of well-informed advocates in the research community:

> The methodology for RCTs is one of the greatest intellectual achievements of the 20th century. It has allowed the development of much of modern medicine and it is likely that it will remain a key way of finding out what works indefinitely. ... RCTs are characterised by an elegant simplicity. They aim to answer one question – whether the thing being studied makes a difference – by excluding all other potential explanations. (Forrester, 2012: 442)

Praise indeed and Forrester has a point. Back to gastric ulcers, once the argument that the bacterium *H. pylori* was their most common cause had finally won the day, the RCT could take its bow. Only through this rigorous testing has the current treatment of choice, a combination of acid suppressing medication and two or three different antibiotics, been established. If we had a gastric ulcer we would be jolly pleased our treatment carried these credentials. RCTs, because they are interested only in what works, not why, are potent eliminators of bias. Forrester has similar aspirations for social work:

> Randomly allocating families to [a family centre] and to 'normal service' and then following-up their welfare would provide a much stronger measure of the impact of the Centre – because other explanations would be excluded … if there were positive differences we could be fairly confident in concluding that they were a result of the Family Centre's work. (Forrester, 2012: 443)

Forrester is right to assert that social work, in the UK in particular, has been slow to adapt the RCT for its own purposes, and adaptation is vital for social work settings. For example, it is difficult to conceive of a double blind RCT in social work: people obviously know whether or not they are attending a family centre, and indeed whether they are working in one. Furthermore, there is always a problem with context dependency, will an intervention 'port' to other locations – it works here but will it work there (Cartwright and Munro, 2010)? This conundrum also applies to a range of other approaches, for example, it seems actuarially based risk assessment models like Children's Research Centre-Structured Decision-Making (CRC-SDM) can be applied only with caution outside of their original setting.

> Recently published research suggests that unless careful attention is paid to the way in which such structured models of assessment are implemented, they could impair professional development (Gillingham, 2011). This refers specifically to the fact that although such SDM tools are intended for use alongside professional judgment, the day-to-day reality in terms of their actual implementation may be quite different. (Barlow et al, 2012: 72)

It may be that the iterative research-led process of developing and honing an intervention in a specific setting is at least a significant factor in its success.

Notwithstanding these concerns, applying techniques from RCTs like random allocation may provide robust evidence which can have a political influence. For example, these methods have the potential to evaluate practitioner-led initiatives. Indeed, task-centred casework followed this very trajectory into orthodoxy (Reid and Shyne, 1969).

So far, so good for the RCT. It gets a place at the table, but we must be mindful that its cloak of neutrality can conceal political intent.

> The first RCT of social work examined intensive long-term social work for teenage boys 'at risk' of delinquency and followed them up for some years. The boys and the workers talked very positively about the service, but on the key measures relating to crime, employment, and other outcomes there was either no difference or the children receiving the intervention did worse. (Forrester, 2012: 443)

In same sentence the promises and the pitfalls of RCTs in social work are made manifest. What counts as an outcome? Who decides what a 'key measure' is? At what point in time do we measure 'change'? How long do families get 'on the programme', before their 'outcomes' are measured? Blewett and Tunstill (2013) dub this 'outcomes theology', noting its effect on policy and practice:

> The evaluation and the measurement of outcomes has been an increasingly powerful driver of policy development in child welfare for the last two decades. Its importance has been underlined by high profile and costly major national evaluations such as the National Evaluation of Sure Start, commissioned by government which concluded after twelve years of outcome measurement. ... However its 'postponed' ability to draw conclusions from input ironically serves to emphasise the importance of understanding *what services are doing now working for today's children and families ... and how can providers change as they go'*. (p 1, emphasis added)

The Sure Start evaluation is a case in point. The selection of outcomes deemed relevant was critical, the most recent evaluation (Meadows, 2011) found that local programmes cost £4,860 per child but delivered quantifiable 'economic' benefits less than 10% of this figure. Sure Start 'fails' to ensure that children have the building blocks to be 'economically active' future citizens. Yet, crucially, *families* do appear to have gained. Evaluation of family support activities within Sure Start revealed here-and-now benefits in 'coping' and 'caring' (for example, Tunstill et al, 2005; Featherstone, Manby and Nicholls, 2007; Frost and Parton, 2009) but for the counters in their counting houses these outcomes do not count.

The current moral settlements on what should be done with 'troubled families', or 'children at risk' turn these highly political questions into self-evident social goods. Of course we must improve parenting; of course we must have people off welfare and in paid work; of course family placements are better than residential care; of course children are better off in permanent adoptive placements; of course we should not prop up poor parenting; of course we need robust timescales in the family courts, the child cannot wait! These statements are unchallengeable. The invisible hand of defensive routine, no public debate, no challenge, no professional or organisational risk.

But these are contestable, political and moral matters, whichever methodological approach is taken, and RCTs do not neutralise the choices. Bias is inevitable where interventions are moral. We may wish the world were simple, but it is not. This does not mean that RCTs have no place, with adaptation they may help with our understandings of a variety of social work approaches, but RCTs in social work will never be like RCTs in medicine. In the US (and, as we shall see, increasingly in the UK) the reign of the RCT has become inextricably tied up with legitimating of professional activity and the allocation of resources. So much so that areas of activity such as therapeutics have become steadily colonised and the interventions treated as though they are analogous to pharmacological regimens. Moreover, the kind of 'theory-sceptical' empiricist asceticism espoused by US academics, such as Bruce Thyer (and Myers, 2011) further delimits available vocabularies upon which we may fruitfully draw to address the contestable emotional, moral and ethical questions which necessarily saturate social work.

Child and family social work and the drug metaphor

Social interventions are not drugs, and we would do well to heed some lessons from decades of psychotherapy process research in the US, where the dominant paradigm has been dubbed the 'drug metaphor' (Stiles and Shapiro, 1989; White and Stancombe, 2003). This views therapeutic interventions as comprising 'active ingredients' (for example, interpretations, confrontation, reflection, and so on), which are supplied by the therapist to the client, along with a variety of 'fillers' and scene-setting features. If a component is 'active' then 'high levels' within therapy should predict more positive outcomes. If this is not the case then the 'ingredient' is assumed to be 'inert'. The problems with the drug metaphor are as follows and it is easy to see why they also apply to social work activity.

1. It assumes that process and outcome are readily distinguishable from each other, that is, that outcomes are a direct linear product of therapeutic process. In pharmaceutical trials, drugs can be manipulated independently of the patient's condition, but in therapy, process components may reflect changes or 'outcomes' which have already occurred, or are the result of a life event not directly related to the therapy.

2. It makes assumptions about 'dosage'. That is, that 'active' ingredients of specific therapies remain constant, regardless of who is practising the therapy and their relationship with the patient – an assumption that Stiles and Shapiro deem 'absurd' (1989: 527).

3. Despite the very real differences that exist between various kinds of therapy in relation to theoretical orientation, techniques and interviewing practices, the outcomes for patients appear to be very similar. This 'equivalence paradox' (Stiles et al, 1986) again calls into question the notion of linear change based on a number of variables which can somehow be isolated from the therapeutic relationship. This, as Forrester notes, is one of the vexing problems of RCTs in social interventions for drug misuse, known as the 'Dodo bird effect'.

> The Dodo bird effect is the finding that often when credible therapies are compared, they have the same impact: they *all* seem to work. It is named after the Dodo in *Alice in Wonderland* who stated that 'everyone has won, so all shall have prizes. (Forrester, 2012: 446)

4. The drug metaphor ignores the effects of the communicative practices of the client (Stiles and Shapiro, 1989). Clients are not inert. They make contingent choices about what they introduce as a topic for discussion, what they conceal and what they reveal. We can multiply this effect exponentially for child and family social work, where parents in particular often have very good reason to conceal a great deal.

Despite the problems in the use of RCTs in psychotherapy, they remain the gold standard at the top of the hierarchy of evidence. So, why is it that researchers persist in paring down an activity so bound up in communicative practices and so self-evidently laden with contingent social meanings and matters of relationship and trust, to a set of 'ingredients', ostensibly separable from their medium of transmission? Under the current policy regime on both sides of the Atlantic 'demonstrating effectiveness' has become essential to securing and sustaining funding. In many senses, as we have already said, this is perfectly right and proper, but social work activity is not reducible to outcome and neither can process and outcome be clearly separated in all cases. The demands of policy are producing a version of practice, which cannot in reality exist.

A range of time-limited, targeted, (ostensibly) evidence-based interventions, which are frequently part of costly franchises, are 'policy preferred'. These generally incorporate an expectation of 'programme fidelity'. This is a spectacular case of the tail wagging the dog. If the intervention is to be evaluated using the preferred methodology (the RCT) then active ingredients must be identified and only the active ingredients count. The medium and context of delivery are irrelevant. Science is very good at bracketing and disregarding those things it cannot understand or explain. For example, when the Human Genome Project found that only 2% of the DNA in the human genome was amenable to current explanation and scientific utility, the remaining 98% was duly deemed 'junk' (Rose and Rose, 2012: 32). So it is with the 'fillers' in family interventions: we do not know what they are, they are something to do with 'relationships' we cannot put them in a manual, we cannot sell them to credulous governments – they are junk.

Social work and policy-based evidence and the economic imperative

> He has been eight years upon a project for extracting sunbeams out of cucumbers, which were to be put in phials hermetically sealed, and let out to warm the air in raw inclement summers. He told me, he did not doubt, that, in eight years more, he should be able to supply the governor's gardens with sunshine, at a reasonable rate: but he complained that his stock was low, and entreated me "to give him something as an encouragement to ingenuity, especially since this had been a very dear season for cucumbers".
> (Jonathan Swift, *Gulliver's Travels*)

It may be argued that the historical conditions which facilitated the ascent of evidence-based practice (EBP) in medicine were not so much clinical as financial. At its simplest the imperative was not primarily the desire to correct error, but to control resources. EBP provides a handy rationale to accomplish a shift from implicit to explicit rationing of health care. For example, it is clear that during the 1980s, the Conservative government of the time was under considerable pressure to contain costs. One mechanism for so doing was to limit the freedom of doctors to prescribe and treat. Hence, the introduction of the technologies of general management, such as delegated budgets, 'cost improvements' and clinical audit. All these are now well established in social work through the commissioning paradigm.

However, once the criteria by which 'evidence' was to be evaluated were established these forms of research also open up reliable sources of funding for researchers. Many 'encouragements to ingenuity' are produced simply by commitment to a method, but the method, not the phenomenon of investigation must be king. This methodological fetish has arguably reached its high watermark in the UK government commissioned Allen Reports (Allen, 2011a and b) into early intervention. With good intentions, Allen's reports represent the pinnacle of the cost effectiveness, commissioning paradigm. No doubt understanding its potent rhetorical force, Allen's arguments are predicated on economics. Services must yield to interrogation by the RCT and only the RCT will count as evidence. The algorithm recommended by Allen to guide government funding of early intervention services demands that services be evaluated by at least one Randomised Controlled Trial or two quasi experiments. If your service has not been evaluated using an experimental design, it will be quickly culled.

Allen is aware that this formula may jeopardise many UK home grown services and interventions, privileging those from the US in particular where the experimental paradigm is most definitely paradigmatic. His answer to this problem, however, is to prescribe for UK services better 'experimental' methods. The interventions must be made to fit the method, not the other way round. This is not science, it is dogma.

> Like many UK Early Intervention programmes, Nottingham Life Skills has been evaluated many times, always with promising results, but it will need to use a method, such as randomised controlled trial, to meet the standards of evidence used in my review, devised by internationally renowned practitioners such as Delbert Elliott and Steve Aos.... This evaluation would produce the specific estimate of impact on children's social and emotional health that is fundamental to the kind of economic analysis required for public and private sectors to feel confident about investing. What the Nottingham Life Skills programme currently lacks, in common with many other excellent UK–designed Early Intervention programmes, is an 'effect size', which

the economists can plug into their models used in advising investors about where to get the best return of their scarce resources. (Allen, 2011a: 77)

So, Nottingham Life Skills works, except it does not. Allen seems unaware of the changes that would need to be made to the Nottingham Life Skills project to make it amenable to an RCT and the resources necessary to make this happen. He is keen to invoke the experts, but in so doing he manages to gloss over the nuances of their own positions. The following is taken from an online interview with Delbert Elliott, director of the Center for the Study and Prevention of Violence at the University of Colorado which is noteworthy for its nuanced humaneness and critical perspective on the timescales imposed by the very commissioning paradigm of which Allen appears so fond.

> Unfortunately, the whole mechanism for funding these programs is not good. The grant goes for three years and then the program goes away. That's why we're in Montbello, to try to get the agencies to continue the funding after the grant ends. The opposite side is that no program works 100 percent of the time. The discouraging part is that there are kids who go into the programs and come out the other side and nothing has really changed. The issues tend to be environmental conditions they have to live with that could be changed. The heartbreaking part is that it doesn't have to be that way. If we could commit the necessary resources, we could change their lives. (http://connections.cu.edu/news/five-questions-for-delbert-elliott/)

The trouble is one cannot design an RCT for those kinds of community based interventions, nor for simple forms of 'ordinary help'. In fact the more ordinary and relatively cheap the help, the less likely it is to yield to experimental methods. In particular the imperative for 'programme fidelity' jeopardises the supple adaptability needed to help families facing multiple problems. This is underscored in a recent evaluation of the Westminster Family Recovery Project (Thoburn et al, 2012: 235):

> Our conclusions do not support one of the key premises that underpinned the original *Think Family* tender documents (and still in evidence in some recent English government initiatives (Allen Report, 2011), that experimentally evaluated 'model programmes' requiring programme

fidelity should be central to service provision. At least with respect to work with very troubled families who are either 'hard to engage' or 'hard to change', we conclude that the lack of flexibility in this approach risks impeding family engagement.

Furthermore, Thoburn et al note the importance of ordinary practical help with finances and housing, for example. In so doing they underscore our points above. What counts as valid knowledge has a direct effect on what counts as a valid service. So what are we to do as a profession about the distorting effects of the politics of research?

Thus far we have painted a picture of research as highly socially mediated and indeed potentially oppressive, and it is. However, social work is arguably particularly snookered in comparison with other professions. The first reason for this, as we have outlined, is that governments of every hue want to fix families, fix them for good and take the credit. The second is that governments of every hue search opportunistically for 'evidence' to support the latest fix. The third is many researchers search opportunistically for funding opportunities. However, a very important aspect of this murky mess is the absence of a learning culture and a very low level of research literacy in many if not most major social work agencies. There is also very little critical distance on fashion and fad from the inspectorates who are so powerful in driving organisational priorities (see Chapter Five). So, having cast research as a hydra we are now going to argue that it is, or can be, your friend and a critical tool in resisting policy made evidence.

Researching your own domains: research as practice in 'learning organisations'

Social workers and managers must be able to do more than digest bite-sized research summaries – as we have noted above, laminated sheets of research nuggets should be handled with care. For example, social workers are particularly exposed to vade-mecum 'take away' versions of psychological theories of various kinds. There are a number of obvious examples. The versions of attachment theory made available to social workers often lack the equivocations and caveats of the original works (Taylor, 2004). Indeed the simplifying 'lens' effect is often intentional as Howe et al argue:

> [T]heories help to organize what we know. Theories also provide an economy of effort. They allow conceptual short-

cuts to be taken. If the theory is powerful one, it might only take a few observations to locate a particular phenomenon as an example of a class of objects or behaviours ... Hypotheses help to guide future observations, the results of which aid practitioners in further testing and refining their initial assessments and observations. (Howe et al, 1999: 228)

'Knowledge to go' provides just such powerful theories, but contra Howe et al, we do not think that is a good thing. Imagine for a moment Arnold Gesell (for example, Gesell and Ilg, 1943) undertaking the seminal experiments that led to his classification of the ages and stages of cognitive and sensorimotor development in infants. In his laboratory work he observed any number of variously compliant or recalcitrant infants with the aim of charting what most infants do at various developmental stages. Of course, for each of the behaviours he eventually mapped, there would be a good many infants who did not display the behaviour in question for any number of reasons, yet these variations are obscured in the line drawings he eventually produced of children doing what most children did, which in turn populate various professional textbooks. These texts do not invite scepticism, they invite categorisation. They may be good places to start the processes of observation, but they are only the beginning. Thus, social workers need a different relationship with knowledge much more akin to scholarship. They need to be much less reverential about what they read – they need to be more active as Nussbaum describes with aplomb:

> Books are not "alive" ... they certainly cannot think. Often, however, so great is their prestige that they actually lull pupils into forgetfulness of the activity of mind that is education's real goal, teaching them to be passively reliant on the written word. Such pupils, having internalized a lot of culturally authoritative material, may come to believe that they are very wise. ... So, books when used in education, must be used in such a way as to discourage this sort of reverence and passivity. (Nussbaum, 1997: 34)

This requires a shift in conceptualisation of social workers as knowledge users to social workers as knowledge makers. There is an intrinsic affinity between the activities involved in analysis and assessment in social work and related processes in research but this connection is not always made and rarely articulated in organisations busy with service delivery and the ever-present distractions of bureaucracy. But, in many important ways, professional practice *is* research. For example, disciplined and rigorous assessment should be treated as small–scale, but powerfully consequential qualitative and sometimes quantitative, enquiry. Conducted well, it will involve a period of immersion in an unfamiliar cultural context, the negotiation and comprehension of different ways of being and doing, the formation of a range of potential interpretations, hopefully a rigorous approach to confronting them with new data, of testing their fallibility or of specifying and refining them. Mary Richmond, arguably one of the first 'modern' social workers, writing in the United States in 1922, saw just such a connection and argued that social workers, as disciplined observers, could make important contributions to the social sciences.

> There can be no question that family case workers are in
> an exceptional position to make valuable observations upon
> family life at first hand where they are protected, as they
> should be, from too large a case-load, and where they have
> had the kind of theoretical training in social science and
> practical training in social work which supplies them with
> the necessary background. 'The interplay,' says Professor
> Park,[1] 'of the attractions, tensions, and accommodations of
> personalities in the intimate bonds of family life have up
> to the present found no concrete description or adequate
> analysis in sociological inquiry.' (Richmond, 1922: 227–8)

Obviously one can stretch the metaphor too far, and social workers must act and make judgements often in less than ideal circumstances and be accountable for these actions, in ways that researchers are not. However, just as the quality of research depends on the capacity of the researchers to choose wisely and reflect upon their methods and analyses, so ethical practice depends on practitioners developing their capacity to interrogate how they use and *make* knowledge in their practice. For a good deal of the time busy professionals are not really aware of what it is they are doing as Eraut notes:

> [T]here is a need for professionals to retain critical control
> over the more intuitive parts of their expertise by regular
> reflection, self-evaluation and a disposition to learn
> from colleagues. This implies from time to time treating
> apparently routine cases as problematic and making time
> to deliberate and consult. It is partly a matter of lifelong

learning and partly a wise understanding of one's own fallibility. (Eraut, 1994: 155)

There is a pressing need to develop forms of organisational learning and social work education, which inoculate practitioners against becoming passive vessels into which chunks of knowledge, or the kinds of policy incantations we have discussed above may be poured. There has for the last two decades been a backdrop of service reform which pushes social workers increasingly towards precipitous bureaucratic categorisations – a tendency exacerbated by the implementation of poorly designed electronic recording systems (see Chapter Five) and the artificial timescales of the commissioning paradigm.

Obviously social workers need to be taught things, but they need much more. For example, by acting as qualitative researchers of their own practice and examining the way they talk and write about children and families, social workers may be encouraged to explore how formal knowledge gets used in practice and what is the relationship between certainty and uncertainty (Taylor and White, 2000). Similarly, as we noted above vast amounts of data are being collected in the interests of performance management and audit. If we are to nurture a democratic version of the learning organisation these data need to be accessible to practitioners and managers *and comprehensible to them*. Because numbers and counting have become new sources of potential blame in a target-driven culture, and because practitioners cannot easily interpret numerical data, vast reservoirs of information on pattern and difference remain inaccessible. Again, this can be remedied by putting research skills at the centre of education and organisational culture as they are, for example, in medicine.

So research is important for practice in at least three ways:

- Social workers and managers need to draw on published research studies to help them to understand children's and families' needs, matters of safety and risk and to plan their interventions.
- Social workers and managers need to develop research skills, such as observation, synthesis of information and analysis so that they can 'increase the sum of knowledge' about a particular family's circumstances.
- Social workers and managers need to use research skills to examine their preferred theories, their own assumptions, patterns and irregularities in their responses and as a check on the essential but fallible intuitive judgements.

Only when these are embedded in social work education and in organisations can we hope to have a learning culture.

Our final words in this chapter are to stress the apparently paradoxical imperatives to be bolder, more critical, more confident and more modest all at once. We have a new version of command and control in the form of payment by results, as articulated in the Allen Report with its hierarchy of evidence. We must be able to challenge boldly with our own methodological rigour and sophistication. At the same time we must learn to be more critical of intoxicating and glamorous emergent ideas such as the handbook versions neuroscience with their shiny Technicolor brain imagery, but most important of all, we must learn to be more modest about what is knowable and what is not, since a great deal of resource is spent serving the pretence of certainty. The families and children with whom we work exist in complex systems with multiple change agents. If we want to know about their lives and what affects them, we need to ask them. There is only so much the state can know about the operation of systems, as this Director of Children's Services notes:

> 'The trickiest thing is not seeing if the performance indicators are moving, it's knowing if what we've done is making any difference. Yesterday we had the teenage pregnancy stats. Across the country in 2007 teenage pregnancy rose by 2.6% and in Downton it dropped by 15%. What's that the result of? It could be the result of our work, it could be a statistical blip, it could be less young women got legless and didn't have unprotected sex over the course of that year. Could be anything, totally random reasons, could be a butterfly taking off in the Amazon jungle, I don't know.' (Loveless, 2012: 266)

Humility is essential to humaneness.

Note
[1] Robert Park is quoted at this point in order to argue that social workers might fill a gap that sociology had left open.

FIVE

Towards a just culture: designing humane social work organisations

The overall effectiveness of local authority arrangements for the protection of children is inadequate. In February 2009, the Secretary of State issued an improvement notice to Birmingham City Council due to poor performance in safeguarding children and young people. A further improvement notice was issued in September 2010 and during 2011, a major restructure and overhaul of children's services was undertaken with the oversight of the Improvement Board. Since the first improvement notice, Ofsted has undertaken a Safeguarding and Looked After Children inspection and two unannounced inspections of the council's contact, referral and assessment arrangements for children and young people. Concerns with regards to the quality of practice in protecting children have been raised in all three inspection reports (Ofsted, 2012: 16)

Did you hear we became inadequate? We have been in a grief cycle since then. Ofsted has left us running round like headless chickens – we are now going to rush into a restructure. We have not heard much from Munro. I'm fearing that it is going to go into a black hole with Ofsted challenging all the way. I don't feel inadequate, but maybe I am? (personal correspondence with a Senior Manager, in a previously high performing authority, 2013)

That society demands accountability from public services is right and proper. That high standards of practice and service delivery should be expectable is uncontroversial. However, meeting these aspirations in social work services has proved a wicked issue. The quotations above are a stark reminder of the pervasiveness of a blaming culture in statutory children's services which spreads beyond English social work and which has resulted from failed attempts to ensure consistent high standards. The term (and indeed the sensation of being) 'inadequate' is strongly correlated with shame – the primary social emotion (Scheff, 1997). That the inspectorate Ofsted should use this particular term to describe struggling authorities is profoundly symbolic of its pernicious and circular effect. In the first quotation, taken from the inspection of the beleaguered Birmingham City Council is illustrative. Despite being under intense scrutiny (at least) since 2009, things are not fixed. If inspection worked, it would surely have worked by now and more inspections would be strongly correlated with rapid and real improvements. They are not. We can see the shaming effect of being described publicly as 'inadequate' starkly in the second quotation. Inspection is currently at risk of crippling the system. Inspections are currently crippling the system as described by Andrew Webb, President of the Association of Directors of Children's Services in October 2013.

> 'It creates an environment in which it is harder to recruit and retain staff. One director of children's services had a relatively stable service with a three per cent vacancy rate in the children's social care workforce. Ofsted judged them to be inadequate and a year later, the number of posts that were vacant or filled by agency workers was 30 per cent. It is hard to see how Ofsted is improving services for children when a direct consequence of that sledgehammer approach seems to be to destabilise the workforce.'[1]

The medicine is making the patient sicker. Simply, the current system is very badly designed for the business at hand. The culture is not just.

The concept of a 'Just Culture' derives originally from work undertaken in safety critical domains like the airline and nuclear power industries (Reason, 1997) and has been adopted widely in the patient safety paradigm in health services worldwide (for example, National Patient Safety Agency, 2011). A just culture requires that organisations distinguish between culpable and non culpable actions, even if the outcomes in each case are the same. The concept of a just culture requires minimally that an organisation has an accessible memory – which means it has to have a mechanism for the honest reporting of inadvertent errors and systemic problems, described by Dekker thus:

> What is it that can make a just organisation a safe organisation and an unjust one an unsafe one? ... It has to do with being open, with a willingness to share information

about safety problems without fear of being nailed for them. (Dekker, 2007: 40)

Let us set a thought experiment.

Grace is a newly qualified social worker, and she has begun work in a referral and assessment team in a large metropolitan borough. She has been asked to undertake an assessment on a child, Daisy, whom the infant school have referred due to concerns about her arriving at school hungry and dirty. The school have referred Daisy several times, but on each previous occasion, the case has not been considered sufficiently risky for children's social care to be involved. Instead the school have been asked to use the Common Assessment Framework to work with the family. This has not been successful as the parents 'will not engage'.

Daisy's mum has just had another baby. On her first visit Grace is accompanied by a more experienced worker and the nature of the involvement has been explained. Things went reasonably well and Daisy's mum has said she has been having some problems recently with her partner, who is drinking a lot. They frequently have no money.

On the next visit, Grace notices a mark on the face of Daisy's baby brother. She is not sure what it is, but he's a very small baby and it might be a bruise. She feels uncomfortable looking closely. There are several family friends present in the house. It is noisy and she has to ask Daisy's mum to speak with her in the kitchen, where the large dog is asleep. Grace leaves the house without enquiring about the mark.

What Grace does now is crucial and will be affected by the organisational systems and culture within which she works. She is not sure what she saw. She can tell herself she saw nothing. She does not need to tell anyone else. Of course, if the organisation has a just culture, she may be able to return, explain she did not have the confidence to ask about the mark in the difficult circumstances in which she found herself and ask for a colleague to accompany her on a further visit to ask for some more information and reassurance. At present, the chances are that Grace does not work in a just culture and that when she gets back to the office her team manager is concentrating on the impending inspection – she is worried that the team has a backlog of cases and that recording is not up to date and there is a rumour Ofsted is coming. Now that inspections are unannounced, it is like this every day. Grace cannot find another team member to talk to as the organisation has moved to an agile working system and nobody has their own desk. Grace never knows who will be in the office when she gets back. She also feels shame – she should have asked the question – how can she ever admit it? She has nobody else to talk to. She does not know the school well, nor the health visitor for the baby, as the team works borough wide and she cannot possibly know everyone. The 'agile' office is located in low cost, but lavishly refurbished ex-industrial property out of town.

Is this safe? Would any reasonable person say this was safe? Is this humane either for Grace, or for Daisy, or for Daisy's family? Daisy's mother cannot come into the office if she is struggling or has no money. She has no way of getting there. Of course, she can attend the one stop shop in the town centre and speak to a customer relations manager. The authority has a single point of access, a clearly identifiable 'corporate front door', but she will not find her social worker there. Not all social work agencies operate like this, some have heroically held back from these 'efficiencies', an increasing number have (re)designed them out, putting humanity back at the heart of their services as we describe in due course. However, aspects of this design are ubiquitous and sadly still growing in number across statutory children's services as authorities seek to make 'efficiency savings'. Before describing a more productive paradigm upon which to draw for designing services for human beings, we must reflect on how we have arrived in the current predicament.

Looking back on Climbié: what went wrong?

Victoria Climbié's death in 2001 sparked the highly influential Laming inquiry (Laming, 2003) into professional and institutional failure, which proved a pivotal catalyst in New Labour's modernisation agenda for children's services. Resulting legislative changes first outlined in the 'Every Child Matters' (ECM) Green Paper (Chief Secretary to the Treasury, 2003), include the establishment of Local Children's Safeguarding Boards, with the responsibility for safeguarding children and conducting reviews on all child deaths, and increased regulation and audit of child protection responses. The government put in place a series of measures intended to enhance information sharing and early intervention drawing heavily on information and communication technologies (ICTs) to support their ambitions (Hudson, 2002). It is difficult to fault Laming's broad diagnostics of the professional and systemic failures that contributed to Victoria's death – they are many and obvious and usually accepted by the main professional actors involved. However, the policy responses have been based on a set of seriously erroneous assumptions. These are summarised below:

1. People need extrinsic motivation to do a good job.
2. Strong top-down management is the key to quality and performance.
3. Standardisation of processes and explicit targets drive quality – 'doing simple things right'.
4. Efficiency is privileged over 'reliability'.
5. Technologies including ICTs are integral to this reform agenda.
6. Errors are a result of professionals failing to *share or record* information.
7. Managing *institutional risk* is the policy priority.

Let us work our way through the first five, which are related. That politicians cry 'something must be done' and 'it must never happen again' when horrific child deaths occur is understandable. However, the post Climbié reforms took place at the height of the command and control culture associated with New Public Management with its regime of 'targets and terror' (see, among others, Bevan and Hood, 2006; White et al, 2010). The first five in our list of errors above are substantially the result of the unholy alliance of public outrage at the death of a child and this insidious regime which was predicated on a pessimistic view of human motivation. This view is seriously at odds with what the research base on human performance in complex domains tells us (Chan and Reich, 2007; Wastell, 2011, Hood 2012a and b). Command and control assumes the need for extrinsic motivation where in fact the credible literature shows strongly that self-set goals to be much more effective in motivating people. If goals in the form of targets are set and performance is measured against them, then 'leaders' who do 'well' are often those attending to the performance regime, not those focusing on optimal system redesign and professional support.

This is perhaps best exemplified in the now notorious Integrated Children's System in which all stages are embedded in software rendering timescales and targets easily traceable by managers, inspectors and all.

The problem with the Euclidian orderliness is that it obscures complexity while creating complication. The workflow model and its ticking clocks concentrate the mind of the human actor on the arrows and the flow. As a result, rather inelegant new verbs have entered the professional lexicon: 'I've outcomed it' (Wastell et al, 2010). The case might been 'workflowed' or 'outcomed' within the system but the real work, whether this is face to face with families, or careful reflection, analysis and synthesis of observations and interviews is subordinated to the imperative to move the case through the electronic system. We might note that despite recent successful critique in England, this model is being exported as we write (see Featherstone, White and Wastell, 2012).

This regime has been critiqued at length by John Seddon (2008), a systems thinker focused on the public services. Seddon is withering about command and control which he dubs 'deliverology', referring to the establishment of the Prime Minister's Delivery Unit in 2001, headed by Sir Michael Barber. Seddon sees Barber as the high priest of command and control, with its belief that all 'change had to be driven by the centre' (p 120). Seddon forensically deconstructs the paradigm, concluding:

> Barber describes deliverology as 'world class tools and processes'. I think of it as Mickey Mouse command and control. That is being generous to Barber and unfair to the mouse. Deliverology's method amounts to determining change on the basis of opinion and driving activity down into systems with no knowledge of the impact on the way the system will perform ... It is tampering on a massive scale ... ploughing onwards with nothing more than a set of plausible ideas, ignoring their lack of success and showing persistence in the face of contradictory evidence. (2008: 117–18)

Barber's method is 'to create a bureaucracy for measuring and reporting that then deludes people into assuming improvements are real' (p 120). This is magical thinking on a national scale (Wastell, 2011), but it is not fairy dust for child and family social work, it has cast an enduring evil spell.

We will not reiterate at length here the empirical findings on the impact of this regime, but see, among others, Broadhurst et al (2009), Wastell et al (2010) and White et al (2010) for the unsavoury details. However, it will be illustrative to our argument here briefly to show one representative data extract from White's empirical work, which gives a flavour of bureaucracy's pernicious effects. Initial assessments (IA) were to be completed at this stage in seven working days: local authorities were inspected against these timescales which, unsurprisingly, were driving practice, but not in a good way (Broadhurst et al, 2009). In empirical work across five local authorities in England and Wales, researchers found an expedient method of completing an IA 'front and back-ing' (or 'back-to-back-ing') had spontaneously emerged across all sites – middle sections of the document were omitted altogether:

> Researcher: So what about the middle of the document, because everyone seems to miss this out?
>
> Social worker: What middle document?
>
> Researcher: You know, practitioners are concerned with the referral and the outcome on the back, but what about all those pages in between about the child?
>
> Social worker: (laughing) To me well ... yes, there is a page about the child, I would always put in something, depending on what the child is like ... I would always put something in, but in IA you wouldn't ... this is initial assessment. (Broadhurst et al, 2009: 12)

Again, we reiterate our question: 'is this a safe system?' Table 5.1, summarises Seddon's typology of durable false beliefs and his various debunkings:

The adage of good system design is simple: if you want people to do a good job, give them a good job to do (Herzberg et al, 1959). The standardisation and micromanagement of process are the result of deliverology, but the glaring delusions of this world view are obscured by moral tales about postcode lotteries, 'timeliness' and the importance of 'compliance'. What rigid processes actually produce is the stripping of requisite variety and agility from the professional response, a point made very clearly in the Munro Review (2011). The Law of Requisite Variety (Ashby, 1956), using the vocabulary of engineering, stipulates that the 'variety' of a 'control system' (in this instance social work service) must equal or exceed the variety of that which is being regulated (families and their troubles). We will return to this point in due course but it is noteworthy that the concept of targets and compliance is so embedded in the management consciousness it is very difficult to unsettle – even when there is an opportunity to design a more appropriate system, the inspectorial paradigm and its facile proxies for 'goodness' may be quickly self-imposed.

The quest for standardisation continues and whether this is through consistent 'thresholds' or 'timescales', it is the wrong approach. Thresholds

Table 5.1: The fallacies of targets

Belief	Seddon's debunking
Targets make people accountable	Yes, they do and people behave accountably. But who should be held accountable for the fact that achieving targets actually makes services worse. The accountability bureaucracy serves the hierarchy ... [it] interferes with the way services work
It is impossible to run services without targets	Wrong again. It is essential to run services without them – instead using measures derived from the work. Many managers are incredulous when first introduced to systems thinking ... working without targets is such a challenge to their mental models.
The alternative is ambiguity and fudge	Wrong. The alternative is clarity and utility. Using measures derived from the work in the hands of people who do the work leads to better control and continuous improvement. Gaining knowledge and understanding is anything but ambiguity and fudge.

Source: Wastell (2001: 100-4)

are dynamic: they bend in response to demand and resources, and are affected by a range of human, social and organisational factors (Munro, 2011; Platt and Turney, 2013). For example, proper analysis of the system demonstrates that as referral rates increase the number of 'non urgent' cases allocated falls (Broadhurst et al, 2009). In such a system, an immobile baby presenting at the Emergency Department with a fractured skull and no explanation will always make it over the threshold whatever the demand, but most children and families referred to social work services are not like that. A family struggling to cope is also going to struggle to get through the front door of many local authority children's social care services and they are going to struggle harder on some days than others. Yet, a great deal of organisational time is spent crafting 'thresholds' and more waste enters the system as universal services try to second guess responses (Masson and Dickens, 2013). Standardisation is associated with manufacturing industry and here it may well equate with efficiency. If one is manufacturing Guinness one needs to be fairly sure each pint tastes very similar to all the others, but it only has limited value where *reliability* is more important. Social work, like other safety critical domains, needs reliability not efficiency.

The simple and palpable truth is that not all processes can be validly standardised without compromising safety. Technologies for *process*

Figure 5.2: The 'quality broom' metaphor

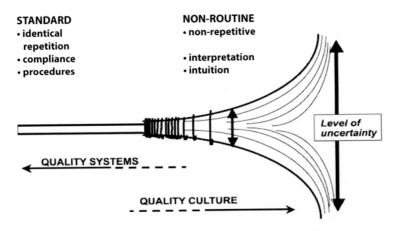

STANDARD
- identical repetition
- compliance
- procedures

NON-ROUTINE
- non-repetitive
- interpretation
- intuition

Level of uncertainty

QUALITY SYSTEMS

QUALITY CULTURE

Source: Based on Lillrank and Liukko (2004); modified with the authors' permission

management will only be effective for routine processes and it is vital to distinguish between these and non-routine counterparts (Wastell, 2011). Put simply, we should not try to standardise processes that cannot be standardised. Lillrank and Liukko (2004) capture this distinction in their 'quality broom' metaphor (Figure 5.2).

Lillrank and Liukko's metaphor shows that standard processes can be managed directly through procedural or technological means, but 'non-routine processes are best managed by indirect means, such as competence, professional values, visions and missions' (p 44) – through culture, in other words (Mannion et al, 2009). Or, as Weick (1987) put it:

'Either culture or standard operating procedures can impose order ... but only culture also adds in latitude for interpretation, improvisation, and unique action.'

Much of the professional task of social work lies at the 'brush' end of the quality broom, which explains in a sweep why standardised business processes were always the wrong approach.

In social work, a routine task may be recording a contact with a service user. Clearly, the child protection procedures (but not the assessment practices) are also amenable to standardisation – they need to swing into action when they are needed in an efficient, dependable and predictable way. However, the work with the family and the sense-making involved in deciding whether a child is at risk in the first place are not amenable to standardisation without compromising safety and system reliability.

The argument, then, encapsulated in the quality broom metaphor, is not for or against standardisation, but for a recognition of the diversity within a system.

> Managers need to decide what should be strictly regulated and what should be left to empowered individuals and groups. ... A great deal of trouble follows, if processes are interpreted as being different from what on closer examination they really are. (Lillrank and Liukko, 2004: 45)

Indeed it does.

Attending to what matters: human factors in children's services

So, we have described the pretty grim status quo, but what would a well designed, humane system look like? To answer this we need to attend to two separate but related matters. The first is what Seddon (2008) calls 'value demand' (providing the service that people want), distinguished from *failure demand* (demands caused by services failures, or wasteful practices). Reducing failure demand by doing things right in the first place is his primary lever for improvement (p 72). Seddon's approach, the Vanguard method, has been successfully applied to children's services in a number of local authorities in England and Wales. The researchers note:

> Cases [often] re-presented at a later date (up to levels of 70% repeat demand in one authority), often after further deterioration in circumstances. In turn, this high level of repeat demand was misleading managers into believing that there was just too much demand to be dealt with, thus justifying higher thresholds for care and support. ... In the redesigned systems, new locally derived measures were instead based around the measurement of a) how well social workers were understanding the problems they encountered, b) the timeliness of the intervention, and c) whether they were able to intervene and stabilise the situation 'right first time' so that these cases did not re-present to the system at a later date. Even though the government had publicly withdrawn from the imposition of central targets, managers in the system remained conditioned to create their own. (Gibson and O'Donovan, 2012: 1)

Social work services, using this metaphor, must thus be designed against demand, by understanding what children and families want and need. Going back to our thought experiment. What did Daisy, her parents and brother need? They did not need an expensive system for saying no (to multiple referrals from school), they did not need a quick and clean execution of a stage in a workflow and they did not need a system distracted by rigid proxies for performance. An inquiry into the child protection system in England conducted by the Education Committee of the UK parliament in 2013 recognised this clearly:

> We were impressed by the evidence we saw of the change in attitude, coupled with a change in structures, which is leading some local authorities to abandon the concept of a threshold for services in favour of a more integrated model in which all children receive appropriate help: what was described to us as the 'you never do nothing' principle. York children's services operate a similar 'no wrong door' policy which means that all cases are examined and offered support. Early indications are that models where a front-door triage service is conducted by social workers in conversation with other partners, *before* any decision is taken on what action to take in response to a referral, is proving effective in directing referrals appropriately, reducing caseloads, and enabling some service to be offered to all children in need, at different levels. This is not a silver bullet to solve all problems. Indeed, one of the consequences to emerge from the evaluation of the Devon model is that workloads for early help teams have increased and that a better range of services is needed at this preventative tier. (UK Parliament, 2013: paragraph 189)

The second set of matters to which we need to attend in designing systems are the so called 'human factors' involved in the primary task. Systems need to be designed for the right species – social work is delivered by human beings, working with other human beings and it is received by human beings. It is instructive at this point to revisit some of the evidence given to the Laming inquiry. In July 1999, Dr Schwartz, consultant paediatrician at Central Middlesex hospital, examined lesions on Victoria's body. Her clinical opinion was that the marks were self-inflicted due to intense itching from a scabies infection. This opinion differed from a previously expressed and documented diagnosis by a locum registrar, who produced detailed body maps of Victoria's injuries and was of the view that there was a strong possibility that she had been physically abused. While Dr Schwartz testified to the inquiry that she had made it clear to social services that she could not exclude physical abuse, the production of a medical explanation for some of the injuries proved a highly consequential red herring. The contact with social services to inform them of the 'change' of diagnosis was made by Dr Dempster, a junior doctor unfamiliar with social services and the child protection system.

Dr Dempster followed up several unsatisfactory conversations with the following letter:

> 'Thank you for dealing with the social issues of [Victoria]. She was admitted to the ward last night with concerns re: possible NAI [non accidental injuries]. She has however been assessed by the consultant Dr Schwartz and it has been decided that her scratch marks are all due to scabies. Thus it is no longer a child protection issue.
>
> There are however several issues that need to be sorted out urgently:
>
> 1) [Victoria] and her mother are homeless. They moved out of their B & B accommodation 3 days ago. 2) [Victoria] does not attend school. [Victoria] and her mother recently arrived from France and do not have social network in this country. Thank you for your help.' (cited in Laming, 2003: 251)

The letter's communicative *intention* was to prompt a visit to the hospital by a social worker, but was read by social services as a recategorisation of the case, triggering a quite different organisational response. Brent Children's Services had two initial assessment teams: referrals were considered first by the duty team, and if the referral appeared to relate to 'a child in need', the case would remain with them for initial assessment; if there were child protection concerns, it would be transferred to the child protection team for urgent action. Thus, within the assumptive world of Brent Social Services, the crucial line of this letter becomes 'Thus it is no longer a child protection issue' and not the documented 'urgent' social matters. The case thus entered a bottleneck in an over-stretched duty team, dealing with backlog of 200–300 cases a week. While these circumstances are clear, such formal organisational systems escaped Laming's criticism; indeed, he prescribes more of them (White, 2009a).

If we examine the events at Central Middlesex from the point of view of the human actors, it is clear that complexities arise from the need to pass what might be speculative and ambiguous information across service boundaries. Communications within a system are embedded in a range of interpretive dichotomies, signal/non signal; information/ noise and pattern/randomness (Serres, 2007). One reader/hearer may find information where another detects only noise. For the receivers of the referrals, the categories 'non accidental injury' or 'child protection case' were the signal, the genuine deliberations of the doctors simply noise. There were plenty of instances of information sharing in the Climbié case, but signal and noise were frequently confused. This is because the players were acting as individuals within the institutional rationalities of their own organisations and professions. Calling an ad hoc assembly of different professionals a 'team around the child (or family)' does not make that collection of individuals a team.

> [S]imply installing a team structure in an organization does not automatically result in effective teamwork. Effective team performance requires team members' willingness to cooperate for a shared goal. … Moreover, effective teamwork depends on effective within-team communication and adequate organizational resources and support. In short, teamwork requires team members to develop a shared awareness of one another's roles and abilities. Without this awareness, serious but avoidable adverse outcomes may result from a series of seemingly trivial errors that effective teamwork would have prevented. (Baker et al, 2005: 10)

The honest appraisal of the effect of service organisation and design on relationships between professionals and in turn on communication and knowledge sharing is essential for safe, humane practice.

Research shows that knowledge sharing is influenced by multiple interpersonal, social and organisational factors, including the inhibitory impact of separate knowledge domains, social hierarchy and low trust (for example, Cross and Borgatti, 2004). Information throughout child welfare is thus 'slippery' (difficult to codify) and 'sticky' (difficult to share across boundaries). The problem is not readily responsive to exhortations to 'share information' (Swan and Scarbrough, 2001; Reder and Duncan, 2003). Yet, this is exactly what the post Climbié reform agenda prescribed. The system was not working to support safe practice, yet the prescription was a stronger dose of the same medicine – a rigid workflow, cumbersome forms and centrally imposed timescales.

If we refer back to our list of erroneous policy assumptions, we must now address number 6, the notion that failures in the system are primarily the result of professionals failing or share or record information. We are not arguing that these things do not matter, or that they are not frequent features of cases that end catastrophically, but they are not in our view usually causal. They appear to be so because the crucial other questions are never addressed:

> Looking back, something will always be found which would seem to provide advance knowledge of impending catastrophe. *But to be sure that this evidence is decisive, we need to know how often it was present in other cases but did not lead to calamity.* Designing on the basis of retrospective correlation is a recipe for disaster, intrinsically linked with magical thinking, but unfortunately in the domain of child protection it is the norm. (Wastell, 2011:176, emphasis added)

The death of (Baby) Peter Connolly in 2007 and the media attention it garnered opened the Laming reforms to renewed scrutiny. Peter was a 17 month old infant, subject to a child protection plan, supervised, like the Climbié case, by the London Borough of Haringey.

> Both the hospital and the social work staff were too willing to believe the plausible accounts the mother was offering to explain child A's injuries. In the more holistic context of the case the explanations offered by Ms A should have been questioned. (Department for Education, 2010: 47)

The quotation above is taken from the Serious Case Review (SCR) into Peter's death. Throughout professional involvement, Peter continued to sustain multiple injuries, as the SCR panel reports above. His death took place years after the implementation of the Laming reforms, which were to ensure that 'this could never happen again'.

So, how *could* it happen again? How can apparently reasonable and motivated staff make repeated errors in the attribution of cause and effect and fail to see what was happening right under their noses? An examination of the literature on human factors in decision making shows this to be not very surprising at all: the post Laming reforms simply failed to take proper account of these factors. The intrinsic characteristics of information processing by human beings operates as both friend and foe in social work decision making. At an individual level, we are equipped with an innate apparatus to assess our fellow human beings on an intuitive/emotional level, and alongside this we have particular cognitive biases. The generation of hypotheses is affected by our cognitive capacities in two principal ways: it is limited by what is *available* in memory, and by 'psychological commitment' to the first hypothesis. This is confounded by the related tendency to seek out evidence that confirms a hypothesis, rather than searching for 'disconfirming' evidence (Wolf et al, 1985). Thus, once we have settled on an interpretation of events we tend to deviate little from our initial 'anchor' hypothesis (Kahneman et al, 1982). In Peter's case, the fallacious formulation was the result of professionals' belief in his mother's account of his behavioural difficulties, including 'head banging', which was also observed by professionals – 'confirmation bias' in action.

When we add to the equation the social psychological and sociological dimensions, which generate powerfully normative cultural practices, we have a heady cocktail indeed (Haidt, 2001; White, 2009b). It is clear that the failures in the case of Peter Connelly were not in *sharing or recording* 'information', but in having the time, space, argumentative flexibility, analytic ability and trusting relationships to debate and make sense of what was being seen and recorded. If we want safer child protection systems we are going to have to design them for the right species.

In England, the range of developments implemented under New Labour described earlier: timescales, targets and the misplaced and misguided pre-occupation with standardisation exemplified in the ICS were to result in a 'perfect storm'. It became apparent that a key casualty of this approach was time spent with families. The audit tail was well and truly wagging the practice dog. Rather than protecting against system failure, these factors exacerbated latent conditions of error (Reason, 2000) because, as we have noted, they made the work bureaucratically *complicated* while failing to take account of its human *complexity* (Hood, 2012a, 2012b).

System design for social work: simple organisations, complex jobs

Figure 5.3 summarises the components of a 'just culture'. If we are going to encourage this in social work agencies, we are going to have design it in. Just cultures cannot be commanded into place (Davies and Mannion, 2013), they need to be grown from the ground. Social work is not unique as a professional activity, though it does have distinctive aspects, and in looking for different ways of designing social care organisations, it behoves managers and policy makers to draw on the literature on organisational design. De Sitter et al (1997) identify mounting uncertainty and complexity as key challenges for all organisations, for which two broad options are available. The first is to increase internal complexity, through the creation of more staff functions and processes and, therefore, more sophisticated management control structures. They dub this the strategy of 'complex organisations and simple jobs' and it is exemplified in the post Climbié reforms to children's services in England. The second response takes the opposite tack, reducing control and coordination by the creation of self-contained units. Fragmented tasks are to be combined into larger wholes, thinking is reconnected with doing – a strategy of 'simple organisations and complex jobs'.

Effectively, the latter response follows a long-established design approach known as sociotechnical systems design (STSD), mentioned above (Wastell, 2011). Several key principles characterise the approach.

Figure 5.3: Components of a just culture

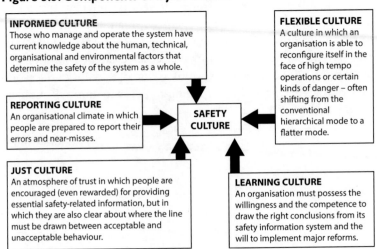

INFORMED CULTURE
Those who manage and operate the system have current knowledge about the human, technical, organisational and environmental factors that determine the safety of the system as a whole.

FLEXIBLE CULTURE
A culture in which an organisation is able to reconfigure itself in the face of high tempo operations or certain kinds of danger – often shifting from the conventional hierarchical mode to a flatter mode.

REPORTING CULTURE
An organisational climate in which people are prepared to report their errors and near-misses.

SAFETY CULTURE

JUST CULTURE
An atmosphere of trust in which people are encouraged (even rewarded) for providing essential safety-related information, but in which they are also clear about where the line must be drawn between acceptable and unacceptable behaviour.

LEARNING CULTURE
An organisation must possess the willingness and the competence to draw the right conclusions from its safety information system and the will to implement major reforms.

Source: Adapted from Reason (1997) and Gain Working Group E (2004)

First, that organisations should be seen as open systems, comprising (for analytic purposes) two subsystems, the 'technical' (technology, skills and processes) and the 'social' (motivation, job satisfaction, organisational and group culture). STSD seeks 'Joint Optimisation' of these subsystems. Put simply, this is a search for a mutually reinforcing balance between what workers need and want, and the technical requirements for effective performance. Other core imperatives include: do not over-specify; and delegate as much as safety and accountability will allow, liberating people to innovate and adapt to unpredictable situations.

There are examples of such redesign within social work, such as the Borough of Hackney's 'Reclaiming Social Work' initiative. Here the 'process paradigm' was seen as part of the problem, not the solution: 'With greater reliance on a procedural approach … a workforce often incapable of professional, creative and independent thinking had emerged' (Goodman and Trowler, 2011: 161). Radical reorganisation along sociotechnical principles (small, autonomous work groups) achieved the virtuous circle of improved outcomes (for example, reduced children in care) at a lower financial cost (Goodman and Trowler, 2011; Munro, 2011). The reclaim model is not the only option and we do not advocate it as anything other than an exemplar. Indeed, much of its success may well be attributed to the fact that it was *designed* in situ not imported. The principles of STSD are important whatever the nature of the organisation. Whether a large local authority or a small social enterprise, designing organisations and systems for the right species is imperative and small is usually beautiful when it comes to the organisation of teams (Stanley et al, 2013).

Organisations must be properly designed, taking full account of both ends of the quality broom. The developments in England at least, over the past two decades, have privileged the management of institutional risk over the improvement of practice. We urge that future developments need to attend to the role of 'trust' in the delivery of human services. Smith (2001) makes an important distinction between trust and confidence. Confidence refers to the general sense of safety and reliability that we invest in systems – having certain expectations in relation to professional roles and the regulatory frameworks governing these systems. Confidence is at the 'hard', handle end of the quality broom, and can be supported by good systems. However, this must not be at the expense of trust, which serves as a guide to interpersonal relationships where the outcome cannot be guaranteed and, indeed, where the possibilities of disappointment and regret are always present – the 'soft' end of the quality broom. If activities such as social work are to bring about positive outcomes in people's lives, then trust is essential.

First, many of those who need services will have experienced situations where their trust was betrayed very profoundly. This might lead to the conclusion that it is better to concentrate on developing systems based upon rights and entitlements. Rights are a vital underpinning for children's services, but rights are exercised in interpersonal encounters and services (including those based upon rights) mediated by people (Smith, 2001). Research evidence suggests that *how* a service is delivered really matters in terms of whether people continue to access it. For example, young people constantly give feedback on the importance of how they are talked to by workers and whether they feel such workers are genuine. Thus, while it is important to measure how many children attend the meetings that are held to discuss their care, it is just as important, if not more so, to devise meaningful measures that assess their level of participation and how they feel about the quality of those meetings. In order for risk to be assessed and change to happen, service users need to tell the truth (Smith, 2001). While this may not always be possible, it is even more unlikely to happen if social workers are not able to build up relationships that are compassionate and truthful in return. Service users value and respond to those who are honest and can deliver the bad, as well as the good news, in a respectful manner. Integral to the building of relationships is that workers have enough time to assess what is happening, to mull over differing versions of events, to weigh up conflicting sets of evidence and to elicit truthful accounts. This kind of work cannot be done by harried workers running from one case to another without the space to think. Good quality supervision is also necessary as the research on human cognition, explored above, suggests we are all prone to cognitive error, particularly when we are tired and emotionally overwhelmed. Supervision should offer a space to challenge judgements made and to process the emotions that will arise when dealing with painful and distressing situations. As we have argued above, as important as the relationship with the families and their individual members, are the relationships with other professionals.

Conclusion

Trust and confidence are related but not the same, and systems that focus only upon confidence building can destroy the possibilities for developing the kind of trusting relationships we have described above. It is time for social work services to grasp the opportunity to embrace principles of system design which aim at building trust and supporting the frontline professional task, guarding against the seductive proxies for quality that timescales and targets produce. These create new arenas for blame and tend to spawn more of themselves in response. There is another way, and here we have outlined some of the ideas that are emerging as alternative principles. As Davies and Mannion note:

> [E]mphasis needs to be on careful local nurturing, reaching for gardening metaphors in place of those rooted in ideas of engineering. Local contexts provide for organic, home grown approaches that are sensitive to local histories and pre-occupations and real change requires detailed and sustained work on the ground. (2013: 3)

Note
[1] www.cypnow.co.uk/cyp/news/1119169/national-children-adults-conference-tough-ofsted-inspections-detrimental-effect-child-services-standards

SIX

Getting on and getting by: living with poverty

Statistics are people with the tears washed off. (Sidel, 1992)

Introduction

This chapter and the next two are informed by a growing social sciences literature on suffering, a literature that not only seeks to engage with people's own experiences but also raises interesting and complicated questions about research practices (Ribbens McCarthy, 2013; Wilkinson, 2005). We would suggest that this literature offers important insights into how vocabularies of expertise have been used throughout modernity diverting attention from the human significance of what suffering does to people (Wilkinson, 2005). Such language is not only ill suited to conveying the existential trauma of human suffering but its tendency towards abstraction has promoted the treatment of people in purely instrumental terms.

This chapter focuses explicitly on the suffering caused by poverty, the lived experiences of those in poverty and the links with maltreatment, while Chapter Seven explores intimate partner violence and the importance of engaging with gendered identities and practices. Chapter Eight draws from research on the lived experiences of families with high degrees of need, vulnerability and risk.

A few years ago, one of us was present at a large international conference on child abuse and heard a very influential researcher deliver a keynote speech about the features that might be present in families where neglect was occurring. The speaker noted that it was often possible 'if one looked around to find a bit of poverty hovering about'. This seemed an astonishing statement from a very well established researcher as it seemed to miss the often all encompassing nature of living in poverty where decisions have to be made often many times a day about what to forego, what to prioritise, and how to stop feeling so ashamed. Indeed, the glib formulation likened the experience to a surface manifestation of dust that could simply be swept away. Such an underestimation or, indeed, neglect is not that surprising and has a recent history in social work (see Becker and MacPherson, 1988).

However, it is problematic and, in this chapter, we attempt to redress what we see as a shocking neglect of the role of poverty and deprivation in families' difficulties.

We explore the insights that have emerged from some of the many excellent studies that have been completed into the lived experiences of those in poverty in the last decade or so. We will argue that a key implication from such studies is the importance of 'ordinary help' for families and the necessity of locating such help within neighbourhoods and communities. We are mindful in this process of rendering visible the strengths that can be harnessed within such neighbourhoods in the service of more humane social work.

Thinking about suffering: representing, colonising, offering 'voice'

Human beings throughout history have been concerned with understanding what suffering means, why it happens and how compassion, particularly towards strangers, can be fostered and sustained. In the 20th century Hannah Arendt is most important in term of her post war analyses. She identified and conceptually delineated a core concern that lies at the heart of all research into social suffering as Wilkinson (2005: 91–3) argues: namely the social circumstances in which people are treated by others, and come to experience themselves as superfluous. She noted that it was in the Nazi concentration camps where individuals were manufactured as 'living corpses' that this was most manifest. Wilkinson argues though it is very important to recognise the ways in which this systematic process of human annihilation originates under social circumstances that are all too readily perceived to be part of the 'ordinary' and 'unavoidable' reality of life in modern societies. Indeed, Arendt identified the treatment of humanity as superfluous as beginning whenever people are reduced to a state, for example, of being 'homeless' or 'socially burdensome'.

Since Arendt, there has been an extensive literature in the 20th century, not surprisingly perhaps, given the horror of that century. A number of studies have explored how some of the most intense experiences of suffering take place as people struggle to negotiate their social identity as 'witnesses of violence' or 'anonymous victims' of devastating disease and grinding poverty (Wilkinson, 2005: 93). Moreover, as we have already explored in previous chapters, others such as Bourdieu have sought to illuminate the 'ordinary' suffering experienced by large numbers of people through years of being socially marginalised and powerless to effect change.

Wilkinson argues that there is a crucial point on which the other studies of social suffering and the work of Arendt diverge: namely, that of how to write of this experience so as to bring it to political attention and policy debate. Arendt sought to fashion a rational vocabulary so as to develop a scientific account of the social conditions under which people come to be treated as 'superfluous human material' whereas other researchers devise emotionally charged language in order to give 'voice' to the personal experiences of individual sufferers. Involving readers in the worlds of sufferers is seen as both possible and desirable. So long as a 'rational vocabulary' dominates our accounts of people's suffering, we will be unable to attend properly to the traumatic ways in which suffering occurs in lived experience.

> Moreover, some go so far as to suggest that where researchers venture to 'translate' experiences of suffering into the theoretical frameworks of social science, then the level of 'symbolic violence' that is brought to bear upon the 'reality' of people's thoughts and feelings distorts the 'truth' of lived experience to a point that is ethically repugnant. (Wilkinson, 2005: 96)

It is argued that the process of writing the details of personal experience in the language of expertise adds to the suffering as it sanitises the 'brute' facts. Kleinman and Kleinman (1991), for example, argue that while economic indicators of suffering may be necessary in terms of rationalising the distribution of resources, this all too often leads to people being treated as problems and instrumentalised.

A key concern for us throughout the next three chapters is that the language that is often used particularly in the policy documents, guidelines and associated research reports not only instrumentalises people but also actually removes them as real live breathing people who are intelligible, need to be understood and taken seriously. Indeed, not making them visible (warts and all) compounds their exclusion and suffering.

Moreover, there is insufficient reflection of the role of research in speaking 'truth to power' and the complexities of undertaking research with those who are suffering. As Hey (2001: 161) notes: 'research is always at some level about seeking and in part claiming an understanding of the other'. Thus, reflecting in a range of ways on whether research practices are complicit in 'othering', exoticising or colonising is vital.

Thinking about poverty

Poverty is a contested term and it is beyond the remit of this book to engage with the extensive literature that has explored its multiple meanings, causes and consequences. We are mindful too that discussion on the definitions of poverty needs:

> to avoid becoming an academic debate worthy of Nero – a semantic and statistical squabble that is parasitic, voyeuristic and utterly unconstructive and which treats 'the poor' as passive objects for attention, whether benign or malevolent – a discussion that is part of the problem rather than part of the solution. (Pichaud, 1987, quoted in Lister, 2004: 2)

The role of researchers, who are often affluent and their responsibilities in relation to representation and/or colonisation, are also the subject of much deliberation with a strong momentum that is, of course not at all straightforward, to involve those who are poor as co-partners in research and in speaking for themselves.

As Lister's own work demonstrates, there have been important developments that have sought to overcome conventional dichotomies between objective and technocratic approaches to measurable income and consumption and participatory subjective approaches grounded in the understandings of people in poverty. Lister (2004) proposes a 'poverty wheel' to represent a relationship of parity and interdependence between the material and the relational/symbolic aspects of poverty. Within the wheel, the material core of poverty represents the hub and this core is referred to as 'unacceptable hardship'. The rim represents the relational/symbolic aspects as experienced by those living in unacceptable hardship.

The literature on inequality explored in Chapter Two is particularly important in highlighting the relational or social aspects of experience. As Wilkinson and Pickett note, inequality has an independent impact on wellbeing. Whether people are happy with their income depends not only on its level but also on how it compares with what others around them have. However, as explored further below, living in unacceptable hardship poses concrete everyday challenges for all members of families affected and these are intensified by, as well as sometimes, ameliorated by services.

Under the last Labour government, ambitious targets were set in relation to child poverty. There was a reduction in the numbers of children in poverty but this progress is now being undermined under the Coalition's austerity programme. While there is a time lag in terms of official statistics reflecting the impacts of policies, there is evidence of an increasing numbers of children and their families experiencing poverty (see Ridge, 2013). This is an important context for this book and makes a chapter such as this even more vital than it might otherwise be, although it would always be relevant.

Money can't buy you happiness, but...?

Ridge (2009) carried out an extensive review of the studies that had been conducted in the previous decade on families' experiences including a raft of studies that had explored the issues with children. Her report comprised a summary of evidence regarding the 'lived experience' of poverty. The following is a summary of the key findings.

She noted the following from the studies with children (pp 2–3). Children were anxious about the adequacy of the income coming into the home and fearful of not having enough for everyday needs. They showed insight into the challenges and demands poverty generated for their parents and anxiety about their parents (for example, in terms of their working conditions or stress levels). They also often tried to moderate their own needs in response to their parents' financial difficulties. Tensions did, however, arise with parents particularly if children were forced into childcare they did not enjoy as their parents worked long hours.

They lacked material possessions such as toys, bicycles and games as well as essential items such as food, clothing, towels, bedding and clothes. Poverty restricted children's chances to make and sustain friendships and the costs attached to getting to, and attending, events as well as holding social events in their homes meant they could not take advantage of social opportunities. Restricted opportunities were also experienced at school, largely, through an inability to pay for resources such as study guides and exam materials. An inability to pay for school trips and other social activities, as well as compulsory items such as uniforms, could lead to conflict with teachers and disciplinary action. Children also reported that they were fearful of stigma and social exclusion and that visible signs of poverty and difference meant they experienced bullying from peers.

An important issue concerned poor housing conditions which could impact on sleeping, studying and health. Homelessness was of concern too for a variety of interrelated reasons. The quality of neighbourhoods could result in lack of safe spaces to play and a dearth of local and low cost leisure facilities. There were differences between urban and rural areas and, as we explore further below, there were particular issues about being poor in areas that are generally affluent.

A range of studies in the decade explored with parents their experiences of parenting under pressure. These included Ghate and Hazel (2002), Hooper et al (2007) and Power (2007). Precariousness was a key feature with equilibrium being destabilised by major as well as one-off events (for example, unemployment, loss of hours of employment, unexpected demands from school). In general, mothers were recognised as bearing the brunt of managing and juggling as individual needs were often sidelined in favour of meeting children's needs. Religious ceremonies and festivals, as well as birthdays, all posed challenges with social imperatives to meet with others and entertain needing to be juggled. There were difficult decisions to be made about buying essential goods or saving for future expenditure. Trying to make money stretch and avoid debt was taxing. There was little access to affordable credit and accessing expensive credit had to be balanced against going without essentials. Money for supervised play and leisure activities for children was difficult to find, but the alternatives when children lived in degraded neighbourhoods was that their opportunities for play were in dangerous or unsuitable environments.

Families in deprived areas had worse housing conditions and greater fears about crime and unsafe neighbourhoods than those in more affluent areas. Families in affluent areas had less access to affordable activities for children and other amenities. Children in affluent areas were more aware of their relative poverty. Parents from middle class backgrounds who had fallen into poverty often had high aspirations for their children but their sense of difference could inhibit their own and their children's relationships with other local families and their use of local resources. Stigma was widespread.

Work could be a key way for reducing family poverty but there were challenges in relation to childcare, travel costs, time poverty. Sustaining work and care was very challenging and, for some, work meant long hours in low income employment and this affected family life. Welfare support was critical but many struggled to negotiate the benefits system and late and missed payments or over-payments could exacerbate stress and financial strain.

One study that is not covered in Ridge's review is a small scale but very rich study of 'marginalised mothers' by Gillies (2007). Many of the concerns of this book in relation to stigma and shame are dealt with in this study but it also opens up important issues around class and resilience that are of real value.

Mothering: engaging with working class mothers' accounts

As indicated in Chapter Two, Gillies' study was conducted against a policy backdrop that had a strong focus on parenting. Indeed, Margaret Hodge (then Minister for Children) stated that: 'Good parenting in the home is more important than anything else to a child's future' (quoted in Gillies, 2007: 4). Parenting was not accepted as an interpersonal bond characterised by love and care. Instead, it was reframed as a job requiring particular skills and expertise which must be taught by formally qualified professionals. Moreover, there was a rather extraordinary weight of expectations paced on poor parents: their own practices should be able to transcend economic realities and should be actively compensatory towards their children. With the right kinds of input, their parenting should equip children to be able to overcome their backgrounds. Fathers, for example, were actively called upon in a project to ensure good outcomes for disadvantaged children, although the exact nature of what they could or should do was left very unclear (see Featherstone, 2013).

Gillies argued, however, that the brunt of these policies was borne by mothers. She highlighted the historically specific and class bound nature of policy and professional constructions of good mothering that were being promoted and the 'othering' of working class mothers. Her research with mothers aimed to convey the complex, situation specific nature of personal understandings and actions and to look at the resources the mothers themselves drew on and provided. The mothers mothered in the context of deprivation and economic hardship. All engaged in a day-to-day struggle to survive and ensure their children were provided for. Each had experienced powerlessness and lack of control as a result of economic dependence (whether on the state or an individual man) and all were well aware of the extent to which their actions were restricted and constrained. However, the mothers coped, while striving for better lives, often taking risks in the hope of improving conditions for themselves and their children. In the face of danger, insecurity and destitution they coped by building a 'ledge' from which they could arrest further freefall and plan a forward trajectory. Some gambled with benefit fraud, others placed a stake in a new partner, while others took on debt. These risks were calculated to bring benefits. However, mothers and their children faced drastic consequences if they misfired (Gillies, 2007: 68).

A key issue from this study concerns the powerful significance attached by the mothers to motherhood and the care they felt and demonstrated towards their children. Gillies found that their commitment and sense of responsibility was often characterised by personal sacrifice and struggle, yet also generated great pleasure and satisfaction. She offers the case example of Kelly who remained dedicated to her children through violence, vulnerability and extreme poverty and, in particular, the very serious after effects of all this on her son. Gillies considered her strength and competence was unrecognised in her interactions with professionals and, a key point returned to below, was that her requests for practical support went unmet.

Gillies uses the interesting concept of 'emotional capital' to help illuminate the classed nature of parenting practices, revealing a contrast between middle class preoccupations with academic performance and working class concerns to keep children safe, soothe feelings of failure and low self-worth and challenge injustice. 'In the context of poverty, vulnerability and failure, working-class children may have precious few resources to draw on other than the emotional capital they access from their mothers' (2007: 142). While we would argue against such a straightforward binary position in that our experience in working and researching in cities such as Bradford makes it clear that immigrant working class families are intensely concerned with academic performance, we think Gillies is helpful in highlighting how differing value systems are linked to necessity or privilege. It is also important to reflect on the implications of Skeggs' (2005) observations echoed by Gillies, that working class women are more likely to refuse victimhood, cover up injury, and endure to display than they can cope.

There are extremely valuable insights to be gained from this study but we would urge caution about the theme running through it that constructs mothers as committed to their children come what may. This may be unhelpful particularly to mothers themselves as it does not admit of the possibility of mothers, or indeed fathers, having very complex feelings towards their children including feelings of negativity or what might be called ambivalence (see Hollway and Featherstone, 1997, and the discussion later in this chapter).

In the next study to be explored, that of Hooper et al (2007), we find important insights into some of the circumstances in which mothers and fathers might not feel positive about their children (or one child in particular) and/or harm them.

Poverty, parenting and maltreatment

Hooper et al's (2007) study evolved from an initial interest in understanding the known association between poverty and the risk of some forms of child maltreatment (physical abuse and neglect), towards a broader concern with the complex relationships between poverty, parenting and children's wellbeing in diverse social circumstances. The project was unique in a number of ways. First, the sample was constructed to enable exploration of the diversity of experiences among families in poverty so it included families living on a low income in relatively affluent areas as well as areas of high deprivation and families from a range of ethnic backgrounds. It also included families with a range of different troubles and experiences of services including child protection services. Second, parents' life histories were explored as well as their current circumstances, social networks and experiences of services and interviews were with both parents (where there were two) and one child. Experiences of a wide range of services were explored.

Some of the key issues that emerged from this study are of central significance to the concerns of this book. Compared to other research on parents in poverty, there were high levels of stress in the sample reflecting the impact of poverty and associated issues such as poor or over crowded housing and also the frequency of other forms of adversity including childhood maltreatment, domestic violence, relationship breakdown, bereavement and mental health issues. The life story approach allowed for the exploration of the accumulation of disadvantage over a life. 'Some life experiences made poverty more difficult to manage and poverty made all other forms of adversity more difficult to cope with' (Hooper et al, 2007: 32).

Parenting was an important source of identity, self-worth and satisfaction for most and an absence of other socially valued roles or sense of identity and self-worth could make it difficult to seek or accept help with parenting difficulties. However, both unresolved abuse and ongoing abuse left some parents really struggling to exercise control and authority over their lives in terms of partnerships, parenting and managing on a low income. Some women who became parents as a result of rape had a particularly difficult relationship with their children. Children with behaviour problems posed particular problems especially in overcrowded conditions. Mothers with histories of childhood abuse and/or domestic violence felt further victimised by children who were aggressive and violent to them and other children and found such children extremely difficult to manage.

Contact with ex-partners was a significant source of stress for lone parents, though some ex-partners offered regular and reliable support with children. Other support networks were affected by poverty and constraints. Men had fewer supportive friends than women and tended to rely heavily on partners. Parents of origin could be very important, although friends played an important and different role.

In terms of the relationship between poverty and maltreatment, as Hooper et al note, there is a known association between poverty and some forms of maltreatment such as neglect and physical abuse. By some definitions poverty is itself a form of child abuse although Hooper et al argue this is too stark and it is important to distinguish between different forms of harm. They argue that child poverty is a form of societal neglect – given the approach taken in this book, it is hardly surprising that we reject the focus just being on child poverty but instead would argue that family poverty is a form of societal neglect.

Their study supports the most common perspective on the relationship between poverty and maltreatment which focuses on stress with social support as a key factor in resilience. This finding needs to be understood in the context of a wider literature from a range of disciplines that points to the importance of social networks in supporting and promoting wellbeing and the reverse (see Cottam, 2013).

Hooper et al found that parents' own experiences of violence and abuse had ongoing impacts on their lives and were interwoven with poverty in a range of ways. Defensive investments in identity as a parent, reflecting lack of alternatives as a result of poverty, are of interest to consider and link with the concerns raised by Featherstone (1999) about the restricted notions of subjectivity afforded women and mothers. It is difficult to make space for women to admit they regret being a mother and/or do not enjoy it. For some women restricted opportunities in education and occupational advancement mean motherhood is not necessarily 'freely' chosen and this is then compounded by rearing actual children in difficult economic circumstances. For such women, other mothers, friends and family members may not be sources of support but indeed sources of condemnation or, if feelings are left unvoiced, sources of guilt or fear.

The 'spoiled' identities associated with poverty and other life experiences could lead to social isolation. The need for recognition and respect, often denied to people living in poverty and those who experience forms of adversity such as violence and abuse, could make children's behavioural problems and, sometimes ordinary lack of respect, difficult to bear or manage. The impact of the bodily experiences of childbearing on women's relationships with children, especially those conceived as a result of rape, was compounded by poverty allowing little relief from such difficult relationships. Children's actions, such as running away or wanting contact with an ex-partner, could impede the capacity to protect especially when social, financial and personal resources were stretched. Finally, services could compound feelings of powerlessness especially when practical resources (such as housing) were not dealt with.

Hooper et al found in discussion with professionals that poverty often slipped out of sight as they focused on drug or alcohol problems and on individual attitudes, values and priorities.

> A limited conception of poverty, lack of resources to address it, and lack of attention to the impacts of trauma, addiction and lifelong disadvantage on the choices that people experience themselves as having may contribute to overemphasising agency at the expense of structural inequality. (p 97)

While we agree with Hooper et al on this, we suggest that it is more complex: structural inequality has complex emotional effects in terms of shame and limited (relationship) choices. Social workers need vocabularies for the internal, the interpersonal and the external structural contexts.

Some forgotten and/or marginalised messages for practice

Given the apparent difficulties in contemporary practice with acknowledging poverty and deprivation, this chapter has focused on the problems caused but it is important also to note resources and strengths. Indeed, it is important to remind ourselves of the complexities of everyday lives in the round – complexities that are not always captured in one-off visits by social workers and researchers. In the next section we look at the literature that has emerged on exploring the possibilities that exist within poor communities in relation to protecting children and supporting their families to flourish. But first let us stress the vital importance of 'ordinary help' – the importance of which is something we all recognise in our everyday lives and yet seems to have become marginalised and/or denigrated in contemporary practice. We also need to be clear here that we consider the provision of such ordinary help to be a vital part of the social work role as it has been in the past and mourn its passing.

An impetus for this book was our discomfort with the model of practice portrayed in the 'hard hitting' (*Observer*, 5 February 2012) documentary series called 'Protecting Our Children' which focused on the practices of social workers and their managers in Bristol. The first programme centred on concerns about a 3 year old, Toby, exhibiting signs of neglect and developmental delay. A flurry of commentary in the press and on the internet followed this programme. Much of this commentary seemed to support Suzanne Moore's (2012) more general observations about contemporary discourses on the vulnerable and poor. She argued that instead of being disgusted by poverty, we are disgusted by poor people with that disgust being tempered only by our sentimentality about children. Analysing media commentary on Toby's parents would seem to bear out her analysis (see, for example, Patterson, 2012).

Many social work academics seemed to see the programme as a tool to rehabilitate the battered image of social workers and show their bravery in difficult circumstances, although others felt the social workers were not decisive enough and swifter action should have been taken with the early removal of Toby by the police (Mahadevan, 2012). By contrast, we were concerned by the apparent lack of meaningful, hands-on, practical support offered to the family with a seeming preference for telling the parents what they needed to do. For example, we watched with distress as the father was repeatedly told to construct a safety gate that he was clearly not able to do. This seemed a far cry from the kinds of humane compassionate practice that we would consider essential in social work and, incidentally, a far cry from our own lived experiences of trying to put up safety gates! (Indeed, one of us lives in a house where we are constantly helping visitors who cannot open or close the gate we have!)

Social work historically has always understood the importance of practical help for people whether in the form of small pots of money or help with transport needs and so on. However, as Hooper et al found, over the past few decades there appears to be a limited conception of the impacts of poverty and the associated issues on people's ability to cope. This is of interest given that this was a period where the Framework for the Assessment of Children in Need and their Families was in place, as this document promoted an ecological understanding of families' needs. However, as Chapter Five graphically describes the possibilities promoted by the Framework ran aground in a landscape of targets, timescales and individualised risk saturated approaches and in a context where child protection social workers were often located in centralised offices miles away from the neighbourhoods they visited ever more briefly clutching forms and protocols.

We consider it vital to rethink the notion of the individual social worker from afar visiting to 'screen and intervene' as portrayed in the

BBC programme discussed above and to discuss the importance of practices of ordinary help that are rooted in working within specific communities and neighbourhoods. There are a number of interlined issues in relation to working in communities and mobilising the capacities of communities.

As Jack and Gill (2010) note, community-oriented approaches designed to improve the conditions in which many families live have been very much at the margins of safeguarding practice although there is a great deal of relevant literature (Holland et al, 2011). Moreover, a host of relevant initiatives at neighbourhood level emerged under New Labour. For example, over a five-year period, one of us was involved in evaluating a local Sure Start programme (Featherstone, Manby and Nicholls, 2007). Here families with varying levels of need and risk were able to work with professionals (who were usually not social workers) in a holistic way. Practical issues such as rubbish removal, action on rat infestation or dangerous play areas were all the subject of concern and practice. The importance of the everyday environment and everyday hassles in living were recognised by outreach workers who often came from the same areas as the families they worked with.

Moreover, parents were treated as people as well as considered in terms of their parenting identities. Thus workers had conversations with them about their dreams and longings, fears and hopes and were able to offer access to activities that were about fun as well as counselling for longer-term traumas.

Other important developments in Sure Start were community allotments in an area where access to good cheap food was problematic and cooking classes were also introduced. Indeed, reflecting on the diverse range of activities that Sure Start local programmes engaged with reminds us of the history of social work. For example, Levine and Levine (2002) note the examples of the settlement houses and the community action agency established in the war on poverty in their contribution to Melton et al's (2002) important book on a child–centred neighbourhood-based child protection system.

In a different piece of research, South Asian fathers in Bradford talked of the importance of safe and fun activities for them and their children provided by the local Sure Start, very necessary in a deprived area with high levels of traffic (Featherstone and Fraser, 2009).

In our experience social workers were not always positive about, or welcoming towards, local Sure Start programmes. Indeed we often found suspicion and hostility towards them – they were doing 'soft' work and/or increasing social workers' workloads through increasing referrals. The focus on thresholds discussed in Chapter Five had clearly distorted priorities and practices and 'real work' was defined in a highly restrictive risk saturated way. Indeed, we noted a 'macho' ethos (from women as well as men) when teaching groups of experienced practitioners about Sure Start and it is interesting, that we, as lecturers, found ourselves defensive about our admiration of Sure Start. Linked to the hostility was envy – this was complex, envy about perceived disparities in resources, about being new, favoured and so on. In retrospect, the often voiced view that those who availed themselves of Sure Start services were not really deserving enough offers a frightening glimpse of a world view that had become intolerant and harsh.

It is of course important to note that such views were not shared by all: we did find social workers who went to work in Sure Start programmes and felt they were at last doing 'proper' social work.

In exploring the potential for practice approaches that work with and in communities, it is important to recognise the strengths that can already exist in specific locales. An ethnographic study by Holland et al (2011) carried out between 2009 and 2011 aimed to explore how children were safeguarded through informal networks and how decisions were made to make formal reports of concerns. How were notions of children as a risk, as well as at risk, enacted within a specific locale? What were the perceived geographies of safety/risk in a neighbourhood? What were neighbourhood experiences and perceptions of formal and community safeguarding agencies?

As they note there is much empirical evidence relating to the prevalence of informal care of children in neighbourhoods across social classes and, as is explored further in Chapter Eight there is substantial evidence of care within family networks. During the fieldwork they became interested in an area of activity they called 'community parenting'. They defined this as the informal, everyday, shared culture of looking out for, or looking after, children within the immediate neighbourhood:

> In Caegoch we noticed several features of activities we labelled community parenting. Parents and other residents said they would 'look out' for other people's children on the estate and trust that others would look out for their children. Therefore they were happy to allow their children to play out on the understanding that someone would intervene if their child was distressed or engaged in behaviour they shouldn't. Adults in Caegoch were thus perceived as willing to intervene to care for, or regulate other people's children. (Holland et al, 2011: 7)

The parents also shared information about risk with each other. This culture of community parenting was aided by social and spatial aspects of the estate. The layout of housing and gardens allowed for easy visibility of children playing in the street. A further socio-spatial aspect was the close proximity of family and kinship networks. There was of course a downside which was that the collective culture could be seen as exclusionary to outsiders or to those who became labelled as outsiders following disagreements.

There was a disjuncture between how the residents felt they were perceived by outsiders and how they understood their own practices. 'Much of the activity appears to residents and those who know the area well as self-evident and visible, but to outsiders the same practices may appear to reinforce stereotypes of unregulated children allowed to wander at will by negligent parents' (Holland et al, 2011: 8). Indeed, the estate had been the subject of dismay and anxiety in sections of the press, and there was evidence of negative attributions in discussions with residents of the other estate that was the subject of fieldwork and from different groups of parents within the estate itself.

The picture of unregulated children, however, contrasts with parental narratives as demonstrated in the following quote from a mother living in most of the most stigmatised streets in the area: 'I wouldn't leave them. They are allowed to go out in the garden. If I am out in the garden they can go the end of the street to my sister in law's or across the road to their godmother's or my niece's cross the road but otherwise they are not allowed to go out on the street' (p 9). This quote illustrates a theme frequently to be found in the research literature, People's accounts both do moral work but also offer valuable insights into the everyday decision making of moral actors. This is important as a feature of our harsh climate is how often those who live in particular areas and/or are receiving state benefits are castigated as living in a world of amorality. Thus, their humanity is stripped from them.

As the researchers note, it is important to recognise the real social and economic problems on Caegoch, strongly exacerbated by high levels of poverty. However, many analyses can overlook the positive aspects of life in such communities. Moreover, we would suggest contemporary individualist models of social work practice do not include a concern with harnessing such aspects to support families to flourish. This has not always been the case however (see Holman, 2013).

Jack and Gill (2010) offer a number of practice examples from the recent and more distant past in order to counter what they consider are essentially individually oriented and reactive approaches by social workers to safeguarding children and young people. One of the first examples was the Canklow Estate Project in Rotherham in the North of England. This involved a model of work known as patch endorsed by the Barclay Report (1982). This model operated on the premise that:

> [an individual] will usually have developed relationships varying from the very intimate to the very distant: he [*sic*] will be in sympathy with some and at odds with others. ... He is part of many networks of relationships whose focus is a local area ... whatever his position in, or attitude to the networks, if he falls on hard time, becomes handicapped or is confronted by acute personal crisis, he will be vitally affected by the extent to which networks can be a resource to him by way of information, practical help, understanding or friendliness. It is these local networks and collective responses that constitute ... community. (Barclay, 1982: xiii)

Patch-based workers in the Canklow Estate project adopted a community development approach that aimed to reduce the pressures on local parents and their children by enhancing the range of activities and informal social supports available to them. A five-year evaluation of the project found there had been significant reductions in the numbers of children in care or on supervision orders and that numbers on the child protection register had fallen to almost zero. The workers had helped not only to increase the levels of informal activities and social supports but also reduced mistrust between parents and workers so that help was sought earlier.

Other projects explored by Jack and Gill (2010) included the Henley project in Coventry. This began by taking a broad view of the factors affecting children's health and safety and aimed: to develop a community which was 'informed and thoughtful' about child protection, emphasising that high levels of poverty, unemployment, traffic and crime provided the context in which most safeguarding concerns and childhood accidents had to be understood. It developed neighbourhood-based family support, community action with young people and positive action to build on the strengths of families and communities.

We must recognise, however, the complexities attached to place and community in our complex and fluid society. Jack (2010) argues that place attachment is commonly understood to be part of a person's overall identity consisting of memories, feelings, beliefs and meanings. He argues that in a late modern/post modern world where tradition no longer defines the individual, people are constantly required to recreate their roles and attachment to place and the sense of belonging and security it engenders can take on a particularly significant role in people's lives. The experience of migration and in particular, forced migration is of considerable importance here. As a host of writers have noted, loss is constitutive of subaltern identities – the loss of one's own place, history, the loss of a sense of the achievements of one's group or class, the loss of valued role models, icons and heroes present or past (Frost and Hoggett, 2008). In promoting the importance of working in neighbourhoods we need to be mindful of the need to engage with considerable diversity and fluidity.

An interesting feature of Holland et al's research was their exploration of the overlapping of different spheres of safeguarding in Caegoch: the informal sphere concerned the residents of the community, the semi-formal sphere included the local community development project and a family and early years' project run by a large voluntary organisation. The formal sphere was the statutory safeguarding sector such as social workers and so on. Holland et al explored qualitative accounts of formal relationships between these spheres such as referrals and informal aspects such as attitudes, beliefs and experiences. There was considerable overlap between the spheres with residents volunteering or working in the community or statutory sector and projects in the community sphere being funded to perform safeguarding services.

Availability and approachability were important in facilitating positive relationships between the spheres. These had spatial, temporal and biographical features: proximity, flexibility around time, trust in people who were known, local and been through difficult time themselves, approachable personal manners and flexibility in terms of scope of services. Thus practical and emotional help could be accessed and was available. These enabling features were often apparent in the informal sphere (between neighbours for example), and were also particularly associated with the community safeguarding sphere but much more rarely associated with the formal sphere (particularly social services). As the researchers note: 'many of the enabling features were met by 'patch-based' generic social work teams … which … have largely been replaced by centralised, specialised teams in most social services departments in the UK' (p 11).

These approaches share an orientation to parents as resources for safety. A particularly inspiring example of the (latent) potential of parents and communities can be found in the challenging context of the residual, protection-focused child welfare service of New York City. Tobis (2013) describes a process by which mothers whose children had been removed into foster care were transformed by self-mobilisation and community action from 'pariahs' into 'partners'. It is a story of how individual parents, mostly black and Latina, living in extreme poverty and having overcome domestic abuse and addictions fought to become stakeholders and thus transformed the system reducing the numbers of children in foster care from 50,000 in the early 1990s to 14,000 in 2012.

> The parent advocates' movement has lifted the pessimism that was pervasive amongst child–welfare affected parents. The child welfare system has responded to their complaints. They have voice and are making a difference. … It is now the broader population's responsibility to join with them, to increase their strength and to destroy the pessimism in the rest of population. (Tobis, 2013: 217)

Conclusion

The following quote from Cottam (2013: 9) is sobering to reflect upon especially when juxtaposed with the discussion in Chapter Five and the preceding sections on the trends towards social workers working from centralised and remote offices:

> Members of the Participle team lived alongside a number of families that our Swindon partners identified as most problematic, staying in empty council accommodation on some of the estates. Eight weeks were spent experiencing the lived reality of the families' lives: doing the school run, shopping on the high street, spending social evenings in the local pub, searching for their children after dark and witnessing negotiations with loan sharks. We also gave families cameras to film things 'we wouldn't know about them' and discovered family members who were keen horse riders, actors, maths whizzes, novel writers and artists. Finally, we sat on their sofas as a succession of policemen, social workers, learning support officers, housing officers and others made their calls.

The findings of this chapter, in its exploration of the lived experiences of those in poverty and facing multiple adversities, lend themselves to the inescapable conclusion that social workers need to change where they are sitting!

SEVEN

Thinking afresh about relationships: men, women, parents and services

When we try, especially at times of pain and crisis, to penetrate the mystery of another mind, we are inclined to picture it as being, not a shadowy mass of contradictions like our own, but a casket containing entities which are clear-cut and definite but hidden. (Iris Murdoch, *The Black Prince*)

The student went swimming in the river one day with his girlfriend, a fellow student. She was athletic, but he was a very poor swimmer. ... She was madly in love with him and tactfully swam as slowly as he did. But when their swim was coming to an end, she wanted to give her athletic instincts a few moments' free rein and headed for the opposite bank at a rapid crawl. The student made an effort to swim faster and swallowed water. Feeling humbled, his physical inferiority laid bare. ... Wounded and humiliated, he felt an irresistible desire to hit her ... and then he slapped her face. ... Love's absolute is actually a desire for absolute identity: the woman we love ought to swim as slowly as we do, she ought to have no past of her own to look back on happily. But when the illusion of absolute identity vanishes (the girl looks back happily on her past or swims faster), love becomes a permanent source of the great torment we call *litost*.[1] (Milan Kundera, *The Book of Laughter and Forgetting*)

Introduction

It is our contention in this chapter that the vocabularies with which social workers in children's services describe relationships have become impoverished. This is a point we have alluded to elsewhere in this book, but here we develop it further. Their motivations for 'choices' made are described as both clear and also suspicious and deliberately hidden. They are failing to put their children's needs before their own. They are choosing to stay with a violent partner. If they are men they are useless or dangerous, or both. We argue here that it is time to resurrect the intensity and the subtle shading of relational life, only by feeling and expressing the 'shadowy mess of contradictions', the feelings of shame and rage, the terror about abandonment that we can hope to have proper conversations, to learn about and improve the lives of adults and crucially to keep children safe.

Some of the terrain is already well trodden. In recent decades a recurrent theme has been that relationship based approaches are a casualty of an audit culture as the focus on targets and timescales is inimical to relationship building. A key concern has been the impact of these upon the relationship between the worker and service user, a concern we share. However, in this chapter, we want to discuss relationships more broadly and intimately. We want to address neglected areas such as intimate partner relationships with a particular focus on those between men and women.[2] We are concerned that although parents and parenting capacity are seen as critical in terms of impacting on children's welfare, an irony of the current policy and practice climate is how little attempt is made to understand parents as people, men and women, mothers and fathers, and what they want from each other and how we can support more hopeful relationships between them. This is an urgent task we suggest given evidence of the levels of violence that are blighting the lives of families (see Cooper and Vetere, 2005).

We also offer some reflections derived from our research on how we might better conceptualise and understand relationships between mothers, fathers and services, a theme to be explored further in Chapter Eight when we consider family-minded practices.

Men and women and their relationships in changing families

Over the past few decades, researchers have sought to understand and explore the changes that have occurred in family life. This has been a highly politicised enterprise against a backdrop of competing claims that strike at the heart of all our anxieties about socialising children, security, loneliness and wider societal well-being. Smart (2007) provides an overview of the debates.

She identifies the longest running debate as concerning whether 'the family' is in decline. This argument conventionally focuses on the behaviours of adults in relation to divorce, co-habitation and birth of children outside marriage.

[T]rends towards heterosexual co-habitation are understood to signify a rejection not just of marriage but also of moral values, which involves avoiding the responsibilities that should attend creating a new family unit. High divorce rates are also interpreted as flight from responsibility, a refusal to work sufficiently hard at relationships and a prizing of individual happiness over collective – or more specifically – children's well-being. (Smart 2007: 13)

However, attempts to refute the decline thesis have been around almost as long as the thesis itself. Fletcher, for example, in 1966 saw the family as becoming more democratic and considered this was founded upon good quality intimate relationships between spouses. He argued that the high divorce rate was indicative of high expectations and refusal to put up with the kinds of situations that people had been forced to tolerate in the past.

There have been many studies since that have contested a fragmentation thesis and stressed continuity and connection across family members. In the main these studies have been based upon in-depth interviews that examine not only living arrangements but also a range of *family practices* and the meanings attached to forms of exchange and connectedness which tend not to be visible at the family survey level. The incorporation of the meanings people give to their relationships has been a particularly important element in these alternative studies. With survey data the researcher often has to impute or guess the reason for visible trends, attending to the 'phenomenology' of family living and family practices adds vitality and nuance to the debates (Smart, 2007: 15). There has been an accompanying clear move in academic study, away from focusing on 'the family' as an institution to exploring practices and fluidity around the meanings attached to kin and non kin.

The literature exploring the changing meanings of intimacy was boosted by the much debated analysis by Anthony Giddens in his book *The Transformation of Intimacy* (1992). He argued that women, aided by feminism, had pioneered a profound transformation of intimacy. 'Personal life has become an open project, creating new demands and anxieties. Our interpersonal existence is being thoroughly transfigured, involving us in what I shall call everyday social experiments' (p 8). In the earlier periods of modernity there was an almost inevitable connection between love and marriage for many women. However, according to Giddens, we are now in the territory of the pure relationship. A pure relationship refers to a situation in which a relationship is entered into for its own sake from what can be derived by each person from a sustained association with each other, and is continued only in so far as it is thought by each party to deliver enough satisfaction for each individual to stay within it. In the era of the pure relationship what emerges, by contrast with the one and only properties of romantic love, is confluent love which presumes equality in emotional give and take. Love only develops to the degree to which each person is prepared to reveal concerns to each other and be vulnerable to the other. Romantic love was bound up with fantasies about the loved one and these fantasies were gendered. Fantasies of invulnerability in men sustained by both partners rested upon women doing the emotional work and carrying men's emotional vulnerability. Thus, it is argued there has been a move in contemporary society towards greater equality which is leading to changing relationship patterns.

Virtually every aspect of Giddens' thesis has been contested. Criticism has come particularly from those concerned to point to the empirical evidence on inequality and violence in relationships (Jamieson, 1998). Moreover, Giddens' complete neglect of children is really problematic as the presence of children is a central factor in why many adults stay in emotionally unsatisfying relationships (Smart and Neale, 1999). However, as Smart (2007) notes, Giddens has argued in response to critics that he is describing an ideal form of family/relationship and one which may come about in the future. Smart also questions whether literal readings are always the most generous or fruitful way of assessing the value of what is anticipatory theorising. Moreover, it is clear that researchers on same sex relationships and new trends in living and relating which are beyond the notion of the family have found his analysis of value with the emphasis on different expectations and negotiation proving particularly fruitful (Smart, 2007).

As noted above, there has been a concern to move away from reliance on survey material and imposing meanings on statistics to exploring lived experiences in families. However, as Smart notes, despite the undoubted strengths of qualitative research, it can be very hard for respondents to talk to researchers about troubles in family relationships and, therefore, the struggles involved in living with family troubles may not always be adequately engaged with by researchers. Nevertheless, this has been an area of considerable methodological innovation. Indeed, in a recent research project, one of us (Dermott, Gabb and Featherstone, 2013) used interviews and weekly diaries to explore with non-resident fathers how they 'do' intimacy. The diaries have offered moving accounts of pain, loss and loneliness. Other research techniques that seem to be proving of value include photo elicitation, eco-maps and digital technology (see also Chapter Eight for discussion of research with vulnerable families).

Giddens' analysis has been used to consider the role of social work in supporting men, women and children to negotiate 'democratic families' (see, for example, Featherstone, 2004a; Ferguson, 2011). For Ferguson such families are those 'where children are heard as well as seen and feel safe, women as well as men are treated with respect, and men as well as women are enabled to have expressive emotional lives and relationships' (2001: 8).

There has, overall, been little research with service users themselves, men and women or same sex couples about what they want from intimate relationships or where they go wrong. This omission is surprising given data suggesting that there seems to be a high degree of fluidity and, indeed, fragility in relation to sustaining relationships. An audit of case files in a project on engaging fathers found, for example, very complex arrangements with high numbers of social fathers and non-resident birth fathers (Roskill et al, 2008).

But we know little of what the figures signify. Are those who suffer multiple deprivations and traumas arising from sexual violence singularly ill equipped, and supported to, overcome toxic histories of distrust? Does it tell us something about women and their desires for more equal relationships? Are women victims of men's flight from commitment or are at least some of them chasing Giddens' notion of the pure relationship? Before this is dismissed, it is important to note Smart and Neale's contention that it may be those who are not enmeshed in property or financial commitments who seem the most marginalised who actually have the freedom to pursue relationships for their own sake. Examining data on intimacy and family struggles, we have a (tentative) hunch that Giddens may have been onto something after all. When a 'pure relationship' is the desired ideal, and money and opportunity are tight, it may create a pressure cooker for anxiety, shame, jealousy and rage.

Since the 1990s there have been concerns, particularly from the Right but not exclusively, about whether the provision of welfare supports women and men in 'undesirable' behaviours with no financial incentives either to enter partnerships or stay together. Others have pointed to the longstanding changes in the economy that have rendered unskilled men's employment prospects much more precarious and thus undermined a key aspect of the historical incentive there was for women to partner. Moreover, a central prop of men's identity has been destabilised with particular implications for men and boys in terms of identities and practices.

There have been linked attempts to blame feminism for encouraging irresponsibility especially among men. By contrast, feminists have pointed to the importance of state support being available to enable women to reject violent relationships.

Children and their relational meaning

An important development in the literature on intimacy has been reflections on the changing meanings attached to children, mothering and fathering. Beck and Beck-Gernsheim argued that, rather than the cool notion implied by Giddens' pure relationship which implies a rational moving on when the relationship no longer meets the person's needs, the love between adults can be desperate and needy but vulnerable and temporary:

> Traditional bonds play only a minor role and the love between men and women has likewise proved vulnerable and prone to failure. What remains is the child. It promises a tie which is more elemental, profound and durable than any other in this society. The more other relationships become interchangeable and revocable, the more a child can become the focus of new hopes – it is the ultimate guarantee of permanence, providing an anchor for one's life. (1995: 73)

There are conflicting views among researchers about children and their significance for men and women (see Featherstone, 2009, for a summary of the differing views). For example, it is argued by some that while there is a general pattern of gender convergence in the desire for fewer children, international research suggests that women want children more than men do. Others such as Dermott (2008) argue that, while parenthood is less central to the construction of adulthood for men than women, it is not clear that fatherhood has lost its significance. Moreover, her research points to the growth in what she calls 'intimate fatherhood': this seems to encompass fathers' desires to have strong emotional connections with their children without necessarily sharing in all the tasks associated with child care.

A key point is that there may be tendencies for men and women to rely on children more than on each other and of the increased importance of an emotional connection with children to both men and women. Beck and Beck-Gernsheim (1995, 2002) suggest that increasing battles post-divorce illustrate the importance to both. Smart and Neale, based on their research into post-divorce family life, would accept there is much that is compelling in Beck and Beck-Gernsheim's analysis. Men's anger about custody laws and their willingness to challenge women legally can be seen as part of a wider process of individualisation through which there develops a yearning for a permanent bond that only a child can supply. However, they argue that it is a weakness in the thesis that the authors do not differentiate between the *perception* of a child as provider of permanent unconditional love and the actuality of parent–child relationships (Smart and Neale, 1999: 17–18). Children, in short, can disappoint and even usurp. Although one is scarcely allowed to think or say this currently, since all behaviours exhibited by children must be attributable to parenting (White and Stancombe 2003), children have different personalities and temperaments and some are easier to parent than others.

In the last chapter we noted a key finding from studies of parents in poverty of the significance of their children. While Gillies (2007) noted the strengths of marginalised mothers' attachments to their children, Hooper et al (2007) noted the difficulties of parenthood being invested in defensively in the absence of alternative sources of recognition and respect. Importantly they noted the difficulties posed by children's challenges to their parents as they got older, and/or engaged in troublesome or violent behaviour towards them.

Interesting findings have emerged as a by product of the many evaluations that have taken place of service engagement with fathers. For example, Featherstone and White (2006) in a small scale piece of research with young men mainly from minority ethnic backgrounds in London found high levels of resentment expressed by young men towards the 'power' that they considered the mothers of their children to have. This seemed to encompass resentment towards the mothers of their children and a wider resentment about women's power more generally. A key issue highlighted by this research was the importance the men attached to the emotional relationship and connection with the child. While mothers were constructed as unreliable or too powerful or both, children were talked about only in terms of love and connection.

Gender, social constructions and practices

Underpinning all these debates are anxieties about gender identities, relationships and the consequence for order and security. The ascription of nature and fixity to men and women has been profoundly de-established practically and theoretically over the last few decades but, of course, continues to be asserted and rediscovered particularly through popularised scientific discourses.

Social constructions argue gender is not an essence or an inner truth and it is not learned. It is achieved and performed (Hicks, 2008). We are continually referencing and improvising a socially scripted performance with parts that were written before we were born rather than fixed essentially at birth. Language does not merely reflect a world of pre-existing men and women but is an integral aspect of 'doing' gender (Burkitt, 2008).

The relational aspect is crucial. As Flax (1990) argued, gender relations:

> ... is a category meant to capture a complex set of social relations. Gender as an analytic category and a social process is relational. That is, gender relations are complex and unstable processes ... constituted by and through interrelated parts. These parts are interdependent, that is, each part can have no meaning or existence without the others. (p 44)

Moreover, the meanings are produced and acted out within a normalising heterosexual matrix.

Over the past few decades a vast scholarship has emerged charting men and women's practices and their relationships as we indicated above. Of importance for our purposes are the endeavours to deconstruct masculinity and femininity and explore masculinities and femininities. This is central in understanding the interplay between gender and other social divisions, such as class, ethnicity and sexuality for example. Men and women are not discrete unified categories but are internally differentiated along power lines.

The recognition of power relationships within and between categories is vital. The feminist social work project in the 1970s ran aground partly because of the lack of engagement initially with the power differences between women. However, looking back now at the attempts by women social workers to establish relationships of empathy and commonality with women service users from today's vantage point can make one want to be a time traveller! The project was scuppered primarily in the name of children's vulnerability as many of us were involved in reminding 'naive' feminists that the children were the most vulnerable and the dangers of molly coddling their (ir)responsible mothers. It is sobering to reflect on how the pendulum was to swing.

A key point of reflection today is the historical evidence that middle class women have often been part of a contradictory project, to distinguish middle class femininity from that of working class femininity, but also to reorder and make working class women more like them. The trope of respectability has been of key significance here. As Gillies (2007) notes, the process has involved both 'othering' and a misrecognition of the values and strengths that are developed in the course of struggle and lack of privilege.

Men were often constructed in those early feminist social work days as the oppressive other (see Featherstone 2004b for a discussion of the complexities and differences between feminists here). Today there is an extensive literature exploring power differences between men. Masculinities scholars have argued that there is a hegemonic masculinity which, to some extent, acts as a reference point for men to judge themselves against often at great cost to themselves. For example, it is usually heterosexual and white as well as securely anchored in economic privilege and with access to institutional power. Scholars have argued that Connell's (1995) notion of hegemonic masculinity is helpful not because it is how men are but because it helps us to understand cultural ideals and influences. A very important issue concerns how men police each other and themselves and how power relations are played out between men.

Featherstone (2004b) has used analyses of masculinities to explore with, and understand, the issues faced by many of the fathers in the families services are concerned with. She argues for the use of the term 'vulnerable' to signify their often very precarious connection to labour markets and histories of abuse and physical and mental health difficulties. Ferguson and Hogan (2004) explore excluded young men's tendency towards a protest masculinity: 'Men's practices of drinking, violence and criminality … constitute a public acting out of a 'hard man' image. Their status and definition of themselves as men is given meaning through protest, an acting out of being against everything that is seen as socially valid' (p 136). Connell (1995) has argued that the growing boy puts together a tense, freaky facade, making a claim to power where there are no real resources for power. However, in their research, Ferguson and Hogan note the complexities here – some of the young men were at ease with non traditional gender roles and nurturing their children. There is a lot of concern with facade which they suggest social workers need to get beyond.

There has long been recognition that gendering practices are central aspects of social work, although there has been a lack of attention to the complexities attached. Mantras such as social workers focus on mothers and neglect fathers are the beginning but not the end of the analysis. In the next section we explore some of the complexities.

Social workers are often women, who by virtue of their occupation, have already achieved a certain level of education and educational privilege often unknown to service users. They visit women in their homes in order to talk to them about their children. Men may be present or absent but, emotionally, will normally be both. There is a literature on the occupational discourses that circulate within social work offices that support constructions of the women visited as oppressed by men but also as ultimately responsible for children's welfare and protection. There are also discourses that support constructions of the absent/present men as dangerous and/or no use. There is also evidence that occupational identity overrides gender identity in that women and men social workers feel much more in common with each other than they do with same gender service users (Scourfield, 2003).

Featherstone and Fraser (2012a) and Featherstone, Fraser, O'Dell et al (2012) found that while gender was never mentioned by either the workers or the service users they interviewed, a range of complex issues emerged that linked to the strong levels of responsibility attached to mothers but most importantly their own expectations of themselves. As mentioned in the Introduction, one mother wept as she explained why she had never been supported to fulfil the responsibilities she wanted to carry: Jenny was a mother of three children who had experienced a childhood of sexual abuse and being in care. She had three children and had kicked out her abusive partner. When she found herself sinking into depression she approached children's services for help and they made her children subject to a child protection plan, an action she described as 'bullying'. Indeed, she described to the interviewer: 'I've been bullied all my life and this is more of it.' Jenny wanted to care for her children but she wanted some help. There can be little sense of a continuum in the services offered especially, as explored further below, in the case of domestic abuse. Responsibility is either all or nothing, or if an action is taken it is wrapped in stigmatising or judgmental language – you are depressed and therefore your children must be at risk. If Jenny contests the assessment, she quickly becomes constructed as resistant or being difficult to engage. Jenny's inner life becomes 'but a casket containing entities which are clear-cut'.

Hasina lived with her husband who drank and had gambling problems and had been violent towards her. Hasina attended every meeting with the social workers and always made the children available so they could see and speak to them. Her husband was angry and unwilling to meet with the social workers and had not taken up the offers of help with his drinking and gambling. There is no doubt this was not an easy situation for anyone concerned. In our research which involved interviews with all the adults involved, it became apparent that because the social workers had focused attention on the mother and not worked with them both together, an impasse had been reached. It is perhaps not that surprising that he resented an intervention that was focused on 'empowering' the mother. While men resist social workers literally by not engaging or disappearing, social workers also 'disappear' men thus placing the women who love them and/or are afraid of them in very difficult situations. Women like Hasina end up being categorised as 'passively compliant', an example of language use that renders the complexities of her situation invisible and also obscures the power/powerlessness nexus she is in.

In our research we have found complex gendering practices by men which render them unable to engage with or be engaged with by social workers. For example, Featherstone and White (2006) found the men invested in a language of rights, thus compromising possibilities for open dialogue with social workers who commonly construct rights talk on the part of adults as selfish or irresponsible. In a DVD made with men as part of the Fathers Matter research project (Ashley et al, 2006; Roskill et al, 2008), men reflected on being unable to make the kind of self-presentation that would help them achieve their goals. They spoke of being judged by their appearance (for example, having tattoos and being big in build) and they also spoke of how they got angry and could not engage in the 'right' kinds of talk. It seems to us that these men are describing something close to shame and we know that a concomitant of shame is often rage (Scheff, 1988). The men in the lives of women and children are living complex emotional lives – they too are more than 'caskets containing entities which are clear-cut'.

As we indicated previously, the tragic death of Peter Connolly provided the context for a whole scale rethink of directions in policy and practice. Here we want to focus on less well rehearsed issues in relation to thinking about men and women. Peter lived with his birth mother but had contact with his birth father. It transpired after his death that two other men were living in the flat who were tried and convicted alongside the mother for his death. This case could have opened up discussion about the complexities of women's relationships with violent and/or dangerous men as this has been a feature of a number of tragedies. It could also have raised issues about why Baby Peter's birth father appeared to be as invisible to services as the men who were hiding in the flat with disastrous consequences. But it did not raise these issues. This fits within a longstanding pattern and is reflective of a culture where child abuse or protection scandals become focused on the actions/inactions of professionals, systems and procedures rather than for example what might be happening in the adults' intimate lives, relationships and psyches.

We are left wondering who, if anyone, had had a conversation with Peter's mother about what her hopes and dreams were, what she thought she deserved in a relationship from a man, what kind of man she wanted to be with. Social workers have become unaccustomed to discussing the 'irrationalities' which form part of human experience; we have arguably lost important vocabularies as a result of the declining influence of psychodynamics in social work (Stevenson, 2013). Social workers focus primarily on behavioural changes to parenting practices, failing to explore what holds destructive relationships in place. For example, what role is played by sex and desire? In the relentless focus on risk and danger, have we lost the capacity as social workers to talk to adults about desire, its seductions and its perils?

Loneliness is also a seriously overlooked issue for many women raising children on their own. Research on a Sure Start project found many women expressed that they missed adult touch as well as company (Featherstone, Manby and Nicholls, 2007). This can be exacerbated by living in which they areas they feel unsafe. Workers in the same Sure Start project told us of women who were afraid to go to sleep at night or kept music on all night to mislead possible burglars, and/or who got a dog and then had difficulty finding the money to feed the dog. For some women, staying with one man no matter how undesirable may be judged the least worst alternative.

In the very limited discussion on the role of the men in the death of Baby Peter, the focus was on the dangers of 'stepfathers', producing a problematic bifurcation between safe birth fathers and dangerous others (Revans, 2009). As Batchelor (2003) has pointed out, methodological problems are rife in the work looking at child abuse and stepparents. Not only is there inconsistency in the definitions of abuse used, there are difficulties around the term stepparent: 'if abuse is attributed to a stepparent, was he or she a long-standing member of the child's household or one of several transient adults in that child's life?' (p 203). As she notes, men who have problems in forming close attachments and who have a history of violent relationships may have a series of relationships with vulnerable women, some (or many) of whom may be single parents. These men may come into contact with and abuse a series of children, any or all of whom may be classed as their stepchildren, regardless of whether they have taken on what may be considered to be a parenting role. Similarly, men seeking to sexually abuse children may seek out and build relationships with single parents as a means of having access to children; their sexual abuse may figure in research as 'abuse by a stepparent'.

Research into child murders by men, with or without the aid of women, suggest the importance of understanding how men and women both made vulnerable by repeated experiences of economic, emotional and psychological deprivation abuse and trauma can be caught up in very damaging relationships with each other. Thus, it is imperative we do find ways of engaging with them as parents, partners and people and abandon our current stance of relying on the mother to protect the child, without ever, it seems, having a proper conversation with her.

Although there is little explicit discussion about men and women's relationships, the issue of domestic abuse has attracted a voluminous research base and literature. In the next section we do not attempt to summarise that literature but rather to point out some of our concerns about how it appears domestic abuse is being dealt with in practice.

Domestic abuse

Awareness of the physical and sexual violence experienced by women within and outside the home, coupled with a growth in understanding about the consequences of many women's economic dependence, has been a key achievement of the women's movement. In the 1970s attempts to get social work to address violence for the sake of women's welfare were to prove unsuccessful. It was the linking of the abuse women received with the implications for children's welfare that was to prove of enduring significance culminating in legislative change and the linkage with emotional abuse.

While there have been some gains, we would argue that the insertion of domestic abuse into a child protection paradigm has been problematic for women, children, men and services. For women, the majority of agency responses have tended to focus on the role of the mother in securing the protection and welfare of the children and encouraging women to leave or to get the men to leave. This is a position that Mason (2005) has called 'unsafe certainty'. While an illusion of certainty is pursued, the reality is that these men do not just disappear, they may hide, they may go onto other families and, moreover, their physical absence does not connote emotional absence in the lives of women and children. They leave traces of yearning as well as pain, traces that may be very difficult for mothers to manage as they deal with their own and their children's sense of loss and disappointment.

We would suggest that we need to engage much more with the women concerned and hear their stories. There is an assumption that the expert knows best but practice may also be informed by an occupational discourse, explored above, identified by Scourfield (2003) in his fieldwork with social workers. This discourse considered men in the families dealt with as either no use, and/or dangerous so, therefore, women were better off without them.

For children there have been some developments in terms of therapeutic support, although these remain patchy. Researchers have noted over the decades that children sometimes blamed their mothers for putting fathers in prison and there was a degree of idealisation of absent fathers (Featherstone, 2009). Such findings underscore the importance of developing systemic understandings and approaches. There are wonderful examples of individual pockets of practice with women and children such as the project run by the NSPCC in York (Radford, 2013). This helps mothers and their children separately and together to explore their complex and conflicting feelings and journey towards healing together. But these projects are in a minority.

There is a history of developing programmes that work with men who are violent to women in intimate relationships although service developments tend to be patchy and there can be a reluctance in times of austerity to develop such resources because of beliefs that scarce resources should be focused upon women and children.

Programmes have usually been named *perpetrator* programmes and have their roots in both the therapeutic, anti-sexist men's movement and the women's refuge movement in the US (Featherstone, Rivett and Scourfield, 2007). Historically, it is the latter that emerged to set standards for treatment and safety as a result of concerns that those with a more therapeutic focus were in danger of excusing men's behaviour. Moreover, they were considered to be too isolated from mainstream services and, therefore, unable to ensure the safety of women and children (Rivett, 2010). The Duluth programme emerged over time as the foremost programme reflecting a feminist perspective on the causes of violence as rooted in men's control and power over women in a patriarchal society and masculine socialisation practices (Pence and Paymar, 1993). It was, and is, designed to be embedded within a coordinated community response and is not supposed to be a stand alone programme. It has its origins in community reaction to the murder of a woman in a specific locale. This history is of relevance in understanding the apparent high level of anxiety about moving away from a set format. Safety planning for women and children is central. It consists of a set format where power, control and equality issues are systematically addressed and where cognitive-behavioural therapies are used. This is the model that has been supported by UK governmental guidance and is the regulated programme for criminal justice settings. Practitioners within the field have created a charity called Respect to lay down standards of good practice and to accredit programmes.

Over the years Duluth programmes have been subject to a number of criticisms. Their set format is considered to be too prescriptive and insufficiently sensitive to the differing needs of differing men attending programmes (Rivett, 2010). An allied critique has contested the underlying theoretical approach as it assumes singular explanations for why men are violent (Gadd, 2004). A linked critique has contested the reliance on cognitive-behavioural approaches and argued for psychosocial approaches that engage with unresolved childhood pain and trauma. A range of writers have suggested the importance of recognising that not all violent men are the same (Gondolf, 2002) and that not all violence is the same (Johnson, 1995). Moreover, it is argued that the role played by factors such as mental health difficulties and substance misuse needs more consideration than that found in Duluth (Rivett, 2010).

The originating impulse of the Duluth model was to explain the violence in singular ways and to see any other explanation as part of men's attempts to excuse or minimise their behaviour. This reflects a tendency towards dichotomising approaches as if one level of description or explanation necessarily excludes another. However, there have always been those from within a feminist politics who have argued against this: 'To say that violence, domination, subordination and victimization are psychological does not mean they are not also material, moral or legal' (Goldner et al, 1990: 345).

In the last decade as a result of a number of developments, men's identities as fathers *and* perpetrators of domestic violence have been highlighted and there has been a growth in interventions that engage with men who are violent as fathers. Featherstone and Fraser (2012b) conducted an audit of interventions in this area. A key reason for the growth was:

> 'Children's services are struggling to get a grip on the issue of domestic violence in families and one of the key problems is that it's such a widespread problem. They're really struggling to find an appropriate response because you know they recognize that they can't take every family where children are exposed to domestic violence to a child protection case conference. So you know sending fathers on perpetrator programs is a very sort of attractive solution for children's services.' (UK academic)

There has been a growth in interest in engaging with fathers and domestic violence also because of changes in public law with contact between both parents seen as desirable even in circumstances where there is domestic violence.

With the emergence of a diverse set of constituencies into this area and the focus on fathering practices, there are tensions apparent. For example, an influential development from Canada has been the 'Caring Dads' programme (Scott and Crooks, 2004). The programme has a both/and philosophy. It relates to men as fathers and as abusers, contains gender reflections and assumes men can change, and explores men's maltreatment of children generally. While the originators of the programme see it as having a 'fatherhood' focus *and* a 'perpetrator' focus, this is strongly contested by those who would emphasise the need to stress the identity of perpetrator as primary and the necessity of adopting the Duluth format (Respect, 2010).

A degree of defensiveness and policing of programmes is evident with strong moral injunctions that experimenting may imperil women and children's safety. But innovation is also evident. For example, Strength to Change is a public health approach in Hull. It works with self referrals and uses a variety of formats and theoretical approaches (Coulter, 2013). Daybreak is a charity that uses a family group conference approach with domestic violence across a number of local authorities using a whole family approach. But the current situation is that pockets of really excellent work are evidently done but widespread systemic interventions are not apparent (see Cooper and Vetere, 2005, for an example of one such project but in a specified geographical area).

It is important to note that, in arguing for the need to address relationships between men and women, we need to clarify that we do not think all can be understood and explained: there are some things that are unthinkable. But we do think humane practice means being able to move beyond some of the rigid and split thinking that is apparent. There is also a real urgency attached to the need to develop local services that engage with men, women and children in integrated ways combining legal, therapeutic and safety interventions. At the moment pockets of expertise in working with different parts of the family are scattered through the system (Cooper and Vetere, 2005).

Conclusion

We want to encourage social workers to engage with the complexities of relationships, to have the kinds of conversations they might themselves wish to have if they were in desperate circumstances. This requires that an examination of 'parenting practices' must become an important part of a more thoroughgoing effort to understand everyday struggles, disappointments and desires. Reporting on an inspiring parental self-advocacy project in New York, Tobis (2013) notes:

> Anyone who has experienced their own difficulties might think about the times we have been depressed, have not had enough money, have drunk too much, or have broken promises to ourselves. Think about the mistakes each of us has made while parenting. (p 217)

If we cannot do this basic empathic and imaginative work, if we cannot have difficult conversations, we are obviously in danger of leaving children in profoundly unsafe situations living with very unhappy adults or removing them without having had the kinds of conversations that might support healing and some form of closure.

Notes

[1] *Litost* is a Czech word which Kundera describes as untranslatable but is similar to shame.

[2] We do not wish to reproduce assumptions that relationships are universally heterosexual here, but simply to make an intervention into the dominant literature that opens up thinking about heterosexual relationships,

EIGHT

Tainted love: how dangerous families became troubled

This chapter examines the ways in which families with complex needs have been understood and represented in policy discourses, and the implications for social work with families where there are care and protection needs. Family-minded practice has struggled to receive sustained attention in social work, and yet the notion of family as the context for the resolution of children's needs extends the scope for supporting change and provides an accurate reflection of children's lived experiences. The maintenance of connections for children with their birth family has been a focus of concern across the range of social work interventions, and the messages from research repeatedly highlight the role birth families play in future wellbeing (while recognising that for some children living with their family is unsafe and untenable). The difficulties in arriving at approaches to family engagement in the care and protection of children have, in part, been a product of our reluctance to go beyond the presenting unit (however fractured that may be), despite the evidence that family networks are fluid, diverse and rarely geographically specific:

> 'do you mean who lives in this house or who is in my family?' (child's mother, quoted in Morris, 2012:12)

In this chapter *family* refers to the extended network of the child, and moves away from narrow notions of immediate carers. Family is a contested term; family theorists have argued that new types of relationships have emerged that make traditional notions of family redundant. Intimacy and individualisation have become preferred lens through which to understand relationships. But, for many engaged in family studies, family remains a useful conceptual tool in understanding both how relationships are organised and how they are sustained. It is well documented elsewhere that much family-minded policy and practice is in reality concerned with parents (in particular mothers) (Morris et al, 2009). Understanding how families are understood in policy and then seeking to locate the social work practice responses in this analysis allows us to consider if our responses to vulnerable families are adequate, or indeed appropriate. By tracing the changing discourses that inform family-minded practice the challenges for families in navigating professional terrain become apparent, and provoke questions about how policy and practice may, at least in part, generate the very problems they profess to address.

From partnership to problematisation

Dale et al's (1986) book on *Dangerous Families* reflected the concerns of the time about families where abuse and harm created a high risk environment for children. It captured the then zeitgeist that to protect children social workers needed to utilise expert interventions based on a series of therapeutic interventions into family life, with these professional techniques controlling and resolving unsafe family dynamics. The text had much still to commend it, being concerned with social work assessment and interaction with families, an area of neglected practice. It explored the relationship between legal duties to protect and therapeutic interventions to reduce risk and promote change. This notion of treatment backed by the force of the law had a set of arguably unintended consequences for children and families in the shape of increasing levels of statutory orders and an over representation of poor, disadvantaged children in the care system (Bebbington and Miles, 1989).

Thus the consequences of these types of highly interventionist social work approaches became apparent throughout the 1980s. The numbers of children who were the subject of formal state intervention rose, but without accompanying evidence of sustained change for children. By responding to families as dysfunctional systems needing interventionist treatment, social work reduced the options available to resolve informally the difficulties families experienced. Research commissioned by an increasingly anxious Department of Health revealed the scale of the problem. Families were being assessed according to local, and at times arbitrary, thresholds (where you lived was a key determining factor in whether your child's name was placed on the child protection register (see Parton, 1991 for a good review of the background to the Children Act 1989)) and a revolving door of assessment, refusal and reassessment developed until at the point of crisis families received too much too late after too little for too long.

The 1989 Children Act sought to address this troubled picture. Using the growing body of research commissioned by the Department of Health to inform the law and policy guidance a fresh approach to families was developed. This proved to be an example of research minded policy arriving at mature decisions, not simply the promotion of favoured evidence based programmes of intervention (see Chapter Five for discussions about the knowledge base of policy and practice). Drawing on the empirical studies that demonstrated the importance of family engagement and the value of responses that responded early to family difficulties the Act placed negotiated family support as central to meeting children's long-term needs. The Act introduced the concept of 'children in need' and with it a set of expectations about support for vulnerable families before crisis points were reached. The Act promoted the upbringing of children by their families, wherever safe and possible, and sought to develop services such as the accommodation of a child as a provision aimed at enhancing family stability and potential to cope. Using Fox Harding's analysis (1997), this era gave prominence to set of policies and legal frameworks drawing upon a perspective described as 'the modern defence of the birth family and parents rights'. Certainly the development of the Act and its associated guidance was influenced by strong lobby groups concerned with family rights to support and representation, and moved away from previous approaches that rested on approaches assuming authoritarian paternalistic settlements between the family and the state.

In reality the implementation of Part 3 of the Act was, at best, sporadic (Aldgate and Tunstill, 2000). The development by local authorities of services to children and families 'in need' was discretionary, and the thresholds for service provision forced families into crisis before help could be accessed. While services were often inadequate and skewed towards protection rather than prevention, practice developments that enacted the Act's principles of partnership between families and professionals received attention (see, for example, the rise of family group conferences, FGCs) and research explored the approaches to and effects of family involvement (Thoburn, 1994).

The New Labour government quickly pulled away from the expectations and intentions of the 1989 Act. The growing political interest in outcomes for disadvantaged children saw consultation documents – such as *Supporting Families* (Home Office, 1998) – begin to embed thinking about 'children in need' within a broader debate about children's wellbeing. The impact of a political understanding of social exclusion on children was beginning to be quantified in these documents, and the strategies for addressing the identified poor outcomes emerged. The needs of children for whom social care services would traditionally have been relevant became part of a broader picture of the analysis of pathways into and out of social exclusion. The children who were eligible for services provided under Part 3 of the Act were being located within a description of children 'at risk' of social exclusion.

The policy positioning of vulnerable families thus moved from being the objects of concerns about individual disadvantage and support, to a role (willingly or unwillingly) as partners in New Labour's social project. The emergence of national, large scale preventative programmes came, in some measure, as a response to a political frustration at the limited progress made in implementing Part 3 of the Act. The primary driver however was analysis of the consequences of social exclusion. Set within the rise of what was described as 'the social investment state' (Lister, 2006; Fawcett et al, 2004), political concern shifted from managing the effects of the market to promoting and mediating engagement, with the end goal of economically and social active citizens. Various theories of social exclusion supported the analysis of pathways that led to what was deemed to be a constellation of poor outcomes including worklessness, poor health, crime and low educational attainment. While the concept of social exclusion is recognised as contested, with Levitas (2005) suggesting different forms and understandings of exclusion can be identified (and indeed the argument for its usefulness in prevention being critiqued – see Axford, 2010) the central role the concept played in the wave of prevention programmes initiated by New Labour cannot be underestimated. Its analysis of the long-term outcomes emerging from exclusionary processes were set out in a series of government analytical reports (PATs) leading to a host of policy initiatives backed by changes in law and guidance.

Within this new paradigm the positioning of the child as a recipient of investment for the future changed the focus of family-minded policy and practice. Analyses of risk and protection factors in relation to children's trajectories began to influence mainstream family policy making (Morris, 2005). The development of preventative programmes such as Sure Start resulted from this political interest in notions of predictive risk (Morris, 2011b). The conceptual framework for prevention adopted by these large scale programmes largely rested on assessments about what was being prevented – the analysis often based on grading needs and responses by severity. Debates within the prevention literature continued to be framed by the desire to delineate needs/problems by intensity (Little and Axford, 2004) or to organise provision by assessments of levels of need and levels of capacity (Sheppard, 2011). Debates centred on typologies of need, with levels being created and services categorised accordingly. This linear view of prevention moved the focus away from any analysis of multifaceted experiences of disadvantage towards simplistic notions of levels of advancing or preventing needs. Family experiences of complex, interwoven disadvantage were overlooked in an increasingly binary analysis of risk and protective factors.

These developments paved the way for the rise of 'prevention science' and evidence based early intervention programmes. The evidence from NECF (National Evaluation of the Children's Fund) and NESS (National Evaluation of Sure Start) that families with complex and acute needs failed to engage with the prevention programmes (and debates can be had about whether the services failed the families (Morris, 2011) or the restricted capacity of the families meant engagement was difficult (Edwards et al, 2006)) led to a refocusing of political attention. Two themes emerged in this new policy landscape: the desire to better target family services (although there was already evidence that targeting was often based on unreliable administrative data (Hughes and Fielding, 2006)) and the need to ensure programmes adopted had a robust evidence base. The 'what works' became increasingly of concern and, as Churchill (Churchill and Clarke, 2009; Churchill, 2012) suggests, moved the policy and practice focus for families away from broader concerns about poverty and exclusionary processes towards finding the right intervention to change individual family failings.

This reflected the broader changes in political discourses about families and parenting, with a shift towards notions of problem families and away from families experiencing problems. So we witnessed the changing positioning of families away from having rights and responsibilities in supporting their children, to the rise of families as partners in a political and social project to, more recently under the Coalition government, the identifying and targeting of a category of families as resistant and failing.

Murray and Barnes (2010), using an ethic of care framework for their analysis (TRACE), suggest the changes in policies for vulnerable families reveal a categorisation of family types. From this we can see the emergence of political narratives that attribute particular responsibilities and failures to specific categorise of families. 'Dangerous families' who pose specific risks to children have been transformed into problem families that present risks to society, to future wellbeing and within this may pose risks to individual family members. Murray and Barnes identify across the policy streams the building of a political discourse about socially excluded and antisocial families. Such families are argued to place significant burdens on the state and to demand an unhealthy settlement between the state and the family – one of dependency, intergenerational transmitted deprivation and poor outcomes. The identification by the Blair government of families that were 'high risk high harm' allowed the incoming Coalition government to build on this narrative and to explicitly target what it labelled 'troubled families'. As social researchers and political analysts point out, the very foundations on which this troubled family initiative is built is fatally flawed. The family data used is partial and inaccurate, and the assumptions drawn from the data are unsafe at best (Levitas, 2012b). But the creation of this image of a tribe of feckless, failing antisocial families is central to the creation of conditions that allow a return to highly interventionist and at times pejorative responses:

> 'That's why today, I want to talk about troubled families. Let me be clear what I mean by this phrase. Officialdom might call them 'families with multiple disadvantages'. Some in the press might call them 'neighbours from hell'. Whatever you call them, we've known for years that a relatively small number of families are the source of a large proportion of the problems in society. Drug addiction. Alcohol abuse. Crime. A culture of disruption and irresponsibility that cascades through generations. We've always known that these families cost an extraordinary amount of money ...'
> (David Cameron, 15 December 2011)

In these swirling debates about who they are and what they cost, the complex reality of family life for families who face almost insurmountable challenges is little understood, their experiences are rarely examined (Morris and Featherstone, 2010) and their voices are rarely amplified. In turning to consider family narratives, the pervasive influence of the new political model of troubled families (with its links back into earlier models of transmitted deprivation) cannot be underestimated, nor its consequences for social work practices.

Family practices and family experiences

Chapter Six discussed how suffering is portrayed and understood, and the challenges of sanitising lived experiences to allow for conceptual discussion to be built. For highly vulnerable families there are few studies that capture or portray the daily challenges of extreme hardship. While work by, for example, Anne Powers and colleagues has traced families' experiences of urban deprivation, studies have rarely focused upon the family practices developed in this harsh environment. For highly vulnerable families caught in poverty, living in communities with few resources and dealing with often chaotic and difficult lives, research has struggled to reflect or represent their lived experiences. In Morris's studies at times families held a picture of 'normal life', something they saw as unobtainable and beyond their grasp:

> 'I'm in the middle of moving anyway, so … it would just be able to go shopping without them all fighting and running off and yeah pulling me hair out, just be able to walk down the street as a couple, as a family, not he's running off that way, he's running off that way, and he's ran over in the garden and you're like, oh no, where they gone! That kind of thing, and be able to walk down the street without one trying to run across the road, yeah just things in my eyes a normal family, do you know what I mean, in my eyes that's what I call normal, walking down the street, being able to walk down the street, but we can't do that, I can't do that.' (quoted in Morris, 2012:15)

This sense of unobtainable ordinariness is further compounded by state interventions that explicitly seek to manage risk rather than provide help:

> 'I think it was XXX had a bump on his head, and social services come out, and when they come out I told them, obviously I needed help with YYY, but they didn't want to know about YYY, they just wanted to know how this bump had come on XXX's head, so it was a bit annoying that sometimes they can come out on another matter, but they can't come and help me if I did need help … And then after that it was left at that, so it was a bit annoying to say that they couldn't help me about anything else, but they wanted to know about this bump, and it like makes you want to pull your hair out, from the fact that you was asking for help but they don't want to help you when you really need it, if you understand what I mean.' (quoted in Morris, 2012: 23)

The absence of relationship building with families, with repeated short-term interventions that were experienced as careless breaking of relationships left families resistant to further interventions and, more importantly, building a narrative about service use that would infuse their responses to further provision and practice:

'... like social services for instance, like when they've been in and out of our lives for so long, they've never been allowed to stay, they've always been involved for six weeks and then cross us off, and like not one of those workers, out of all those workers in the last nine years that we've worked with, the ones like who make out that they're really close with us and they're getting on with us and that, when they get taken off the case and never come back to see if we're coping.' (quoted in Morris, 2012: 26)

'... if somebody else helps and it doesn't work you're still left, you're left with double the amount of work really, you can't do that anyway, why should you do that now, why should you let them.' (quoted in Morris, 2012: 31)

'It makes the kids think oh yeah ... so the next person that comes they don't give them a chance. I think it's more rebellion.' (quoted in Morris et al, 2012: 44)

For families where a child had died as a result of abuse or neglect, this sense of services repeatedly struggling to offer sustained help was compounded by the services then seeking to review their practices:

'I think because I was so wrapped up with my baby and my life I don't really have a clear picture of okay this is how it happened. People were all just coming at me and they were all just saying things and it just seemed like an ongoing process, everything was up in the air, and just, and so looking back I'm like okay could I tell you ... it was almost like a story, like a dream, I know it was real, I know it happened, but it feels, I was so wrapped up, so panicky, so emotional with what happened, it becomes hard then for me to say, oh okay yes, so I knew there was a serious case review because such and such, and things like reading the information, I couldn't even do that. It was only when everything was over that I finally was at a place where I could do it and looking back I was like oh okay so that was why, but it was too late...' (quoted in Morris et al, 2012: 46)

In circumstances where a child has died as a result of abuse or neglect, family systems and/or professional systems have failed to an almost unimaginable degree. Families presented complex narratives about their experiences and loss, regardless of whether their actions (or inactions) had contributed to the critical incidents. But, above all was a sense of irresolvable grief and a desire for change:

> 'Professionals don't grieve like the family do; they just move onto the next case, going from one job to another; for the family it stays forever.' (quoted in Morris et al 2012: 43)

Even in these extreme circumstances families revealed a capacity to respond to professional requirements for learning and to provide important insights into the change needed:

> 'it was obvious there was something broken in the system and we cannot walk away without knowing we've made efforts to fix it, and see it fixed.' (quoted in Morris et al, 2012: 43)

Family narratives suggest there is much we have still to learn about how families experience and function in the context of hardship, and the ways in which social work practice can engage with, work alongside and at times challenge these family practices.

Doing with and doing to: family involvement in care and protection

The fragmented provision of state services in the UK has focused upon the individual, rarely actively including their extended network (Morris et al, 2009). The uncoupling of children from their kinship networks (with this child-centric approach evident in multiple national documents) during the process of receiving protection and support affects their later emotional and psychological health; families are an important connection into a child's heritage, history and identity. The notion of the child as a separate entity, an island, also discounts the potential the family may offer to achieving change for the child. However, the involvement of the state in this private domain (the rights of individual family members to both privacy and protection) remains highly contested, and in the UK runs alongside a political discourse that engages in a process of 'othering' those who fail to conform to expectations about family life and require state interventions to fulfil their roles and tasks adequately (Gillies, 2005; Morris, 2011). Thus families using child welfare services are marginalised both by a historical reluctance on the part of legislators to be seen to interfere in private matters, and by virtue of their needs for help and assistance. Krumer–Nevo (2003) describes such families as defeated families; families who are defeated both by their needs and deprivations and by the services that are meant to assist (Morris and Burford, 2009).

Elsewhere the involvement of the kinship network in child welfare provision sits within different conceptual and cultural frameworks. In New Zealand there is an established history of actively seeking out models and approaches to including extended family in service development, in part as a response to past oppressive state interventions in Maori family life (Doolan, 2007). Doolan, drawing on this New Zealand perspective, argues that:

> Families have a right to participate in decision making about matters that concern them and it is at the point where individual and family liberties and freedom of choice are in jeopardy that the state must make its greatest effort to ensure real participation and involvement. (Doolan, 2007: 10)

As already discussed, in the UK, policies have positioned families to become partners in preventative initiatives, at times through encouragement, at times through coercion. However, the empirical evidence indicates that in reality for front line practitioners it is mothers who are the focus of the services (Gillies, 2005; Williams, 2004): thus, *family* policies in child welfare are experienced as interventions in mothering and the parenting that mothers provide. The involvement of the extended family in decision making remains a marginal UK practice development, beset with concerns about professional skills, the risks such developments pose and the challenges whole family approaches present to fragmented services (Morris et al, 2009).

How families are understood, and how they understand they are understood with notions of deserving and undeserving rights to participation, the potential for exercising responsible citizenship and assumed levels of competency infuse how practices respond to family members' needs. Internationally, there is an emerging body of empirical work concerned with how vulnerable adults and children experience and respond to professional practices (Kemp et al, 2004; Harris and Gosnell, 2012). Internationally, user perspectives and experiences are also informing practice development, with studies examining how families experience and understand interventions, in part in response to the evident harm within those communities historically excluded and marginalised (Ivec et al, 2011). Reviews of the evidence and empirical work suggest that there are common qualities that vulnerable children and adults experience as helpful in promoting an effective working rapport. Familiar themes emerge concerned with the flexibility of the worker, their capacity to be responsive and their abilities to create respectful empathetic relationships that hold a relevance to the lives of those using the services (Mason and Prior, 2008; Evans et al, 2006; Forrester et al, 2007). These ingredients for effective engagement are evident across the findings from a range of service areas including youth justice, child protection, family support and addiction interventions.

Likewise, an analysis of the narratives of families with complex needs who used multiple services generated a set of common reflections about the qualities and practices displayed by the practitioners that families identified as helpful and promoting change (bearing in mind these were families who had highly demanding needs and who repeatedly expressed frustration at the perceived inadequacies of interventions) (Morris, 2011b; Morris et al, 2012). The ability of the practitioner to actively engage the family, or specific individuals within the family, was central to the assessed efficacy of the service. Indeed more so than the goals or intended outcomes of the interventions, which families often struggled to describe, reflecting what Parton summarises to be the central message from an analysis of service user perspectives: the quality and value of the experience (Parton, 2003). But the discreet elements of the engaging practices were less tangible – with families repeatedly explaining that they needed the 'right person' to work with them. The analysis suggested that in family encounters with practitioners there were common attributes that 'the right person' demonstrated, with specific interpersonal and professional skills being identified by family members:

- The capacity to care for the family and to demonstrate this care in their practice
- Providing services in a reliable and trustworthy manner that delivered changes
- The ability to set clear boundaries but to do so in a manner that was seen as appropriate and balanced with good listening skills and an acknowledgement of the reality of family life
- The use of positive regard and building on strengths to work with the family
- Acknowledgement of the challenges facing the family and a willingness to act as advocates where necessary
- The building of self-esteem in family members and their ability to resolve problems using their own knowledge and skills.

This construction by families of the 'right person' was echoed in the accounts of families who had been invited to participate in a review when a child in their family had died or been injured as a result of abuse or neglect (Morris et al, 2012). For these families the practices of those professionals seeking to secure their involvement was crucial in enabling them to contribute their knowledge to the review process. This is a contested area of participatory practice, with tensions concerned with the legitimacy and purpose of involvement. Professionals were engaging with the family in highly charged circumstances, where the death of a child had occurred as a result of adult actions/inactions and/or professional service failures. As in the first study, families valued professionals that demonstrated their care in their practice however difficult the context (and the professionals likewise were able to articulate in their interviews the challenges of humane practice in situations where serious incidents of harm had occurred). Sometimes this was evident in the thought given to approaching the family, or sometimes this was evident in the actions taken:

> '... you know, like even the police officer, my washer blew up on the day, and blew up into flames, and that was before I even knew that she'd died and so I had no washer, I was then told, so the last thing on my mind was the washer or the washing, well she (the family liaison officer) left here with two big swag bags of washing and she took them home, and came back, all the washing done, ironed, everything.' (quoted in Morris et al, 2012: 50)

These particular studies, in common with more general empirical evidence from family studies, pose a set of questions for social work. In positioning families as troubled and damaged beyond repair, policy developments create an increasingly adversarial relationship. Practice guidance talks of the need to 'grip' the family, to halt the spiral of transmitted disengagement and poor outcomes. Yet, families point to the primacy of respectful care in effective relationships with practitioners. The political blame game that ascribes wider social ills to the small number of families with whom social work has a long established tradition of working results in difficult terrain for practitioners. Building relationships with families that can support change in the context of their political and public condemnation and vilification is challenging and at times impossible (Morris et al, 2013). Yet the family studies cited suggest that family policy and practice should give attention to notions of care both within families and between professionals and families, and should seek to extend professional understandings of family practices and their capacity to provide safe care. Sociological developments in understanding family practices (how families do family) has advanced (Finch, 2007; Morgan, 1996), but rarely in relation to highly vulnerable and marginalised families. Practice developments that explore family potential require those engaged in supporting families to be able to articulate their underlying assumptions about how families exercise ethical agency and care in responding to vulnerability and risk. There is a value in arriving at a framework that reveals the assumptions being made, and a need to avoid simplistic, binary analyses of family cooperation/non cooperation as the guide to risk and harm. Within this must sit an analysis of the place and function of care and it is this analysis that forms the basis the concluding discussion.

Conclusion: care in adversity

As earlier discussions identified, a largely politically constructed category of families has been found wanting in the drive towards the production of good citizens. Families that exhibit particular behaviours or characteristics are judged to be risky environments in which to raise children no matter how flawed the evidence is about the data on which these assumptions are based. The inescapable reality facing social workers is an ideological drive towards child rescue:

> 'In all too many cases when we decide to leave children in need with their biological parents we are leaving them to endure a life of soiled nappies and scummy baths, chaos and hunger, hopelessness and despair. These children need to be rescued, just as much as the victims of any other natural disaster.' (Michael Gove, Secretary of State for Education, 19 November 2012)

As is argued throughout this book, poverty and its associated social inequalities generate experiences that render family life at times risky and harmful for children. The political shift towards a rejection of the connection of inequalities with children's lived experiences will, with inevitability, result in a shift towards the removal of the children of the poor into state care. This presents society with a slow burning but chronic set of difficulties. Care is a complex experience for children: without 'the right fit' between the care arrangements and the child, many children's care trajectories are a cause for concern. While for some children care is a positive and necessary option, and for whom family life is unsafe, arriving at positive outcomes for children in public care remains a major challenge for policy and practice (as discussed in the National Care Inquiry in 2013).

The empirical work examining family contributions to the wellbeing of children provides evidence of a demonstrated desire to 'do right' by vulnerable family members, even in extremely difficult circumstances. Not all family members and not all families demonstrate such care. But in areas of practice such as family decision making the evidence suggests that many families, given space and a permissive framework, will arrive at *care* full plans for their children. The research also suggests that even when tragic events occur and family culpability is evident, family members can still proffer learning that can assist social work in devising responses that better meet children's needs.

The opportunity to display this capacity to care is compromised by the impact of austerity. Political judgements about what is good or productive family life are now set within a time of restricted access to resources. Vulnerable families face difficult times, with reduced availability of family support and increased pressure on professionals to intervene early in family life where there are concerns about children's wellbeing. So, for families a double bind emerges: welfare practices close down opportunities for vulnerable families to demonstrate their ethic of care, and, by failing to demonstrate care, families are found wanting. We have previously described this contradictory set of experiences for families (Featherstone et al, 2013) but these are set within a neo liberal paradigm that is extending social and economic inequalities. Changes to social security and to poor families' access to state support will severely test the capacity of vulnerable families to enact in any way care giving and care receiving. Evidence already tells us that family care (such as kinship care) produces poverty and hardship (Hunt et al, 2008).

But care is not the sole prerogative of families. In her second inaugural lecture Barnes (2008) argues passionately for bringing care into political deliberations if socially just outcomes are to be achieved. Likewise, at the point of practice empirical studies have revealed the difference demonstrated care in practice makes in the willingness of highly vulnerable families to engage with practitioners. Families described chaotic and confusing lives, and just as they valued feeling cared for, they resisted practitioners that demonstrate a lack of regard or intent. Families are attuned to and could articulate the difference care in practice made:

'There's people in professions right that because they've got this job of I'm here to help it doesn't matter the fact that you don't give a shit about anybody, now there's people that are in these professions that we know will do anything to help another person, it's not because they want reward, or look at me I've done this, because they, they just do it because they know you need that little bit of help.' (Mother, in Morris, 2012: 30)

As troubled and troublesome families become the focus of muscular plans for state intervention (Casey, 2012), we see social work facing fresh challenges. Pressure to arrive at early decisions to remove children, to plan for adoption and to sever family ties place procedurally determined professional decision making at the heart of meeting children's needs. The past is being revisited, but arguably executed in a more pernicious form. *Dangerous Families* built an analysis at a time when the impact of inequalities and extended understandings of family capacity to care were less well understood. We have since developed a robust knowledge base upon which family-minded practice can be built. But arguably the cyclical nature of family-minded policy and practice is evident with the past patterns of high levels of formal interventions in family life discussed at the start of this chapter being repeated in more recent times. As past experience has taught us, approaches that move social work away from exploring family care and capacity and substitute professional decisions driven by expert analyses result in very particular outcomes for children. In the UK and particularly England the numbers of children entering the care system has risen sharply since 2010. This was driven by professional practices responding to overt political pressures, including the political and media responses to tragic child deaths and the growing prominence being given to early removal and adoption. But this rise in numbers was not matched by success in attempts to enhance the recruitment and support of alternative carers, be they kinship carers, unrelated foster carers or prospective adopters. Children's pathways into, through and out of the care system encounter many barriers to wellbeing. Poor practice and scarce resources result in children losing connections with their families, being separated from siblings, experiencing unsafe care (either through unmanaged return home or within the care system) and running overly high risks of mental health problems, poor education outcomes, criminality and worklessness. Too few resources, poor practice and a systemic lack of care (in a care system) renders children highly vulnerable.

Thus we arrive at a picture where the neglect of care across the domains of practice has resulted in ongoing limitations to family-minded social work. Yet the research suggests social work ignores at its peril the importance of extended understandings of care in seeking to arrive at robust, effective long-term plans for vulnerable children and families.

NINE

Conclusions

> There is a peculiar cycle here: social work investigates
> suspicious populations, but its investigations, or at least the
> findings derived from them, make the investigated appear
> even more suspicious. Investigations provide the warrant
> for future investigations. Perhaps the additional stigma is
> necessary because if social workers are to peer into the
> homes of people who want no part of them, if they are
> expected to visit the poor despite the latter's articulated
> desire to be left alone, they need good reasons. Accordingly,
> the more foreign and perverted clients can be made to
> appear, the more authority social workers have to visit
> and keep visiting. Aggressive social work, a social work at
> war is so much easier with families defined as psychotic,
> sadomasochistic, rapidly multiplying, polymorphic perverse.
> (Margolin, 1997: 98)

In his compelling history of the invention of social work in the US,
Leslie Margolin describes the importance for the project of state
sanctioned social work of constructing the poor as passive and non-
reflexive in sharp contrast to the presumed agency and reflexive
awareness of the better off. We have shown that this process of 'othering'
remains central to the current settlement in child protection work.
Indeed, it is enjoying a vibrant renaissance.

In this context it has been an important aim of this book to reexamine
the language and frameworks used and to address how those currently
used have hollowed out important moral and political issues (Ribbens
McCarthy, 2013) in their neglect of questions such as the following:

- Why do we use the language of the *child* and of child protection?
- What is lost and gained by such a language?
- Why is the language of family and family support so marginalised?
- Who is being protected, and from what, in a risk society?
- Given that the focus is overwhelmingly on those families who
  are multiply deprived, do services reinforce or ameliorate such
  deprivations?

- Is it ethically desirable to focus on rescuing children and leaving their parents behind in a society riven by inequalities?
- Why do we not explore and engage with mothers and fathers as subjects in their own right?
- Why are relationships between men and women as parents and partners so poorly understood and subject to so little rigorous attention?
- Why do we so often hide the suffering that we encounter behind a rational vocabulary of expertise?

We have tried in this book to offer an alternative framework drawing from a diverse set of literatures that encompass moral philosophy, social policy, the humanities, sociology, systems theory and psychosocial studies, and our own research on systems and the lived experiences of those involved with current child protection processes. In our conclusions, we summarise our arguments and offer some thoughts for a more hopeful and humane future.

Why do we need change?

Across many countries there is ample evidence that those who experience child protection systems come from communities characterised by powerlessness and deprivation. In seeking to understand the consequences of this for services we have been influenced by the analysis of inequalities advanced by Wilkinson and Pickett (2009). We have also been influenced by the sociological literature on suffering and the psychosocial analysis of 'double suffering' by Frost and Hoggett (2008). This analysis names the both/and nature of the complexities that are often to be encountered when we seek to recognise our fellow human beings and the consequent ethical and practice challenges: 'Subjects of social suffering may not draw easily upon our compassion if they do not present themselves as innocent victims but as aggressive, resentful or suspicious people whose hurt and loss is directed at others rather than at themselves' (Frost and Hoggett, 2008: 453). We recognise and acknowledge the scale of such challenges: being angry with, as well as for, those we work with can never be easy.

We have argued for the urgency of reengaging with a rich and diverse literature from the humanities as well the more familiar sources in the social sciences. Symbolic interactionists from Goffman (1968) onwards have theorised the subjective experience of social hurt in terms of stigma and shame. Think of the experience of the individual who cannot produce the 'normal' social identity required and is aware that they do not come up to standard because the opinion formed by those making judgements does not stop at presentation but makes moral judgements and imputes certain characteristics. The discrediting of this person affects how they see themselves. As Goffman points out, the stigmatised person shares the same belief system as the rest of their culture. Because the sense of inadequacy is internalised within the individual's own meaning system, shame is experienced privately, personally and as all embracing. Shame equals serious identity damage.

We have argued, based upon our research, that child protection processes compound feelings of stigma and shame. A common complaint, for example, is that social workers either do not turn up for meetings or cancel them at short notice or are invariably late. Toynbee (2003) reminds us of the way time is used and abused by those in power:

> I sat there thinking how low value permeated everything about the lives of the poor. I had queued in the post office to pay the rent, trekked to the only shop that re-charges the electric meter and queued again. Everywhere I was kept waiting and yet my time was precious because, like all the people at the agencies, I needed to get a job quickly. But poor people's time is viewed as valueless. (34)

We have already noted in Chapter One that if fathers were late for a contact visit, it was read by social workers as evidence of a lack of motivation. However, social workers were themselves often late for such visits. This was explained away by reference to traffic problems (Roskill et al, 2008).

We also need to understand how meetings, such as case conferences, that are full of jargon and dominated by professionals are experienced:

> 'If you're there on your own, you don't know if you're causing a bit of ... you could be looked at as not really speaking decently, or whatever; it's hard to say criticism and stuff like that, and to object ... I know you have to go through the chair, or whatever, but it's very hard in a Conference like that to say, "Excuse me, you know, that's not at all true, and can I have a right to say my view here." It's very hard not to get anxious. Whereas an independent person, an advocate, is there to encourage and help the parent to say the right thing.' (parent, in Featherstone et al, 2011: 270)

The research with fathers carried out as part of the Fathers Matter project found fathers that were very aware that they could not make the self-presentation necessary to achieve a hearing, and those who were unaware of the fact that the language they used invalidated them from the start. It is thus urgent, we would argue, that social workers and managers recognise and engage with the causes and consequences of double suffering and adopt a highly reflective approach to the encounters they are engaged in.

We have also argued that much of the suffering that is being encountered by social workers and, indeed, being caused is not being named, but rather being masked by an abstract language of expertise. For example, we have noted how increases in care demand are increasingly welcomed as evidence of 'appropriate' and 'timely' interventions. However, it is concerning that the failure to name increases in care order applications as a source of sadness or, at the very least, even to note that their necessity is regrettable flows from a range of research, policy and practice roads not taken in the past few decades.

We need change because, as Chapter Three argued, the work is highly consequential and we have stopped having the kinds of ethical conversations that we need to have. The lack of debate in our society about the implications of removing so many economically and socially deprived children from their parents in the 21st century is disturbing and is a sharp reminder of how demonised poor families have indeed become. The lack of engagement with our history of system abuse and, indeed, the evidence from other countries such as Australia where multiple apologies have been offered by governments for the forcible removal of children from Aboriginal communities and, more recently, the removal from unmarried mothers in previous decades is concerning.

We need change because, as Chapter Four noted, research evidence has been harnessed more and more in support of early removal in a problematic use of the evidence available. The President of the Association of Directors of Children's Services on Radio 4's *Today* programme on 10 February 2012 noted that an exponential increase in applications of care orders during January 2012 was the result of: 'better understanding the effect of neglectful parenting due to drug and alcohol problems and the physical damage to development and to brain development it can do with very young children.' As we have noted in Chapter Four particularly, the lack of caution about using neuroscientific arguments is of serious concern.

But what counts as valid knowledge has a direct effect on what counts as a valid service and we urgently need conversations about the distorting effects of the politics of research. At the time we write this, we are witnessing a vivid example of the contrasting fortunes of research in the context of legislation. The creation of the 1989 Children Act was arguably a high point in the development of central government responses to vulnerable children and families. There is considerable value reflecting briefly on how the Act was constructed, not least because of the helpful contrast it offers when reflecting upon recent approaches to developing and implementing law and policy for children in need and their families. Developed by a Conservative government within a period when inequalities were increasing exponentially as part of a determined ideological project, it is, therefore, of interest to reflect upon the care with which the Act was developed. Indeed, the process was at odds with other pieces of legislation in that period which were often conceived by businessmen with limited consultation (for example, the Community Care Act 1990). The Act built upon commissioned research that was concerned with supporting better understanding by policy makers and practitioners working with the children and families who used child welfare services and the processes involved. The Act also reflected a considerable period of consultation with those who used the services, with practitioners and with managers and policy makers – alongside academics. In the Act, we arrived at *knowledge informed* law and policy. Contrast this with recent developments in relation to the Children and Families Bill going through parliament at the time of writing, where we have seen inappropriate representation of research to support predetermined policies about responses to vulnerable children (as discussed in Chapter Four). The emergence of arbitrary time lines for care planning, the rise of actuarial tools to measure parental capacity with time limited opportunities for change are, ultimately, concerned with a privileging of child removal and adoption as a preferred outcome for children experiencing risk and harm.

We need change because, over the past few decades, a transactional form of welfare developed. This model is rooted in market reforms with their embrace of centralised bureaucracy, targets and timescales, and emphasises efficiency and a particular and limited form of accountability. Yet, time and again, what service users value and indeed what the research tells us is needed for a good society is something more human, caring, time rich (Cottam, 2011). As we explored in Chapter Five, the kinds of reforms developed in relation to child protection reduced time, took people away from people and were premised on a misplaced faith in technological fixes.

We need change because we have lost sight of what is needed in a good society for its families to flourish. The response by the then minister, Ed Balls, to the death of Peter Connolly was to promise the best child protection system in the world, as opposed to making Britain the best place in the world to bring a child up (Cottam, 2011). We need change because we have developed systems that are more concerned with managing institutional risk than fostering a just culture in organisations so that the kind of social work we are promoting, that which places human beings and human factors at its heart, can be developed.

We need change because more and more we have seen a decoupling of the child from their family in a *child-focused* orientation. This orientation concentrates on the child as an individual with an independent relation to the state, thus ignoring the most fundamental of insights about our relational natures. By addressing the child as a separate entity in the family, the state promotes policies that lead to defamilialisation, as it reduces parents' responsibilities for their children in some ways while expanding them and regulating them in others. Thus the complexities of relational identities – past, present and future – are glossed and a mandate is provided for a child rescue project. Parenting is not accepted as an interpersonal bond characterised by love and care. Instead, it is reframed as a job requiring particular skills and expertise. Moreover, while parenting and parenting capacity are seen as critical in terms of impacting on children's welfare, little attempt is made to understand actual parents, what they want from each other, and for, and from, their children. With the framing of parenting as a job, it is little wonder that the concept of redundancy becomes so freely available. While all parents are vulnerable to the state gaze in such a context, there are particular dangers for those who are poor. Their investments in parenthood may be highly valued by them in a context where they have little else and yet be treated with little care by professionals.

We need change because we have developed a very individualist model of practice, a model that is distanced from families and neighbourhoods often. It reflects and reinforces distance with geographically remote offices and more and more forms and protocols. Thus the strengths within families and communities are not built upon or often adequately recognised.

In summary we would argue that:

- We need to dismantle some of the current settlements about child protection, not because children have ceased to need protection, but because the orthodoxies are masking complexity and making children less safe.

- Children are often uniquely vulnerable, but this does not mean they can be seen as separate from kin and community. If we turn children into sacred objects of concern, we make their lives poorer.
- We must recognise the role of family, community engagement and community development in supporting change for children and those they love and are connected to through blood, history and a multitude of ties.
- We need to use approaches that fulfil our responsibilities to intervene where there is harm without risk becoming the dominant paradigm.
- We need to understand risk as a wider concept than the pathologising of individuals and groups. It is a product of multiple influences and is situational.
- Social work must, fundamentally, be an empirical profession. Compassionate and empirical. Social workers must attend to furthering their understandings of the particular family and individuals immediately before them, rather than glossing families into spurious universals and institutional categories. This requires both rigour and humility.

So towards humane social work with families: a family support project for the 21st century

The Care Inquiry was held over a period in late 2012 and early 2013 and was organised by, and engaged with, a very wide range of constituencies: young people in a variety of care placements, adoptive parents, birth parents, foster parents, residential workers as well as charities, NGOs, civil servants and academics. It was organised in order to support dialogue about the care needs of vulnerable and at risk young people particularly in a context where there was an increasing policy push towards adoption as the gold standard. The evidence gathered from a host of respondents, but most importantly from young people themselves, suggested that systems and practices inadvertently or unwittingly produced a series of broken relationships. The Inquiry revealed the extent to which existing policies and practices work against building sustained helping relationships for children and families, while at the same time espousing a very narrow version of permanence which paradoxically has the potential to sever the relational webs within which real people live.

The final report from the Inquiry recommended that we recognise the centrality of relationships in helping children and families, and that we move on from a profoundly unhelpful privileging of particular forms of intervention and care. Such recommendations may have a 'motherhood and apple pie' feel to them. But with the lustre of science increasingly driving our responses, we are in danger of imagining that new approaches to change for children should be rooted in a sophisticated knowledge of how their brains develop, or of the intricacies of particular practice models or indeed the buying in of whole scale systems change. We have argued that the current appeal to science to solve moral problems is an *ignis fatuus*: it has an alluring glow, but its potency is not always real and it silences debate. The Care Inquiry report asks us to think differently and ironically (given the complexity of the Inquiry's processes and evidence) in some ways more simply (Care Inquiry, 2013).

The emphasis on relationships that emerged from the Care Inquiry finds echoes in the call by Cottam (2011: 141–4) to develop a relational approach to welfare more generally and we would suggest it is of value to explore the five principles she outlines as a general approach to welfare as they would seem to have much in common with what we too are arguing in this book.

Take care of root causes

Cottam argues, as we have done consistently, that the more unequal a society, the worse is every quality of life indicator. Developing humane social work with families in a society that is riven by inequalities is a challenging task and, we recognise, needs to be part of a wider project (see, for example, Jordan and Drakeford, 2012). It is, however, essential that we recognise the need to develop and support approaches to practice that are not about rescuing individual children from impoverished families and communities. Moreover, we need to develop rigorous research on child welfare inequalities (Bywaters, forthcoming) and the consequences of inequalities for children and parents' health, mental and physical, self-harming behaviour and abuse. We need much more robust research based on the lived experiences of those who struggle to survive in a society where they face major obstacles to achieving a life of dignity and worth. We need to stop treating symptoms as causes.

Adopt a developmental approach

Cottam offers an example from youth services to illustrate her points here. She argues that they are about evading risk so they focus on, for example, stopping children taking drugs or getting pregnant. However, young people thrive when they know how to engage with risk and when they are emotionally resilient. This resilience comes through relationships and experiences, so that what is needed are youth services that provide this in community rather than in professionalised youth only spaces. For our purposes, a developmental approach moves us decisively away from individual expert 'screen and intervene' approaches towards more community based and collective approaches. We need to use approaches that fulfil our responsibilities to intervene where there is harm without risk becoming the dominant paradigm. As we have noted throughout this book, a range of differing approaches have been developed within already existing systems, such as family group conferences. However, we have also noted the difficulties with bringing strengths based models developed in particular contexts into a system that is so saturated with risk.

But we need to continue to argue with politicians, media and all the relevant stakeholders about the merits of a system that is rooted in recognising and supporting strengths, is realistic about risk and understands the importance of resilience. As we noted in our Introduction, the idealised notion of childhood as a time of protection and innocence in contemporary Western culture impedes the ability to acknowledge that all families are likely to be troubled and fails to equip children to deal with such trouble when they encounter it and, indeed, this failure may itself exacerbate the impact of trouble.

Be infrastructure light and relationship heavy

In past decades the most cumbersome top down systems of command and control developed as we noted throughout this book. We need to free up the resources locked into these systems and develop relationship based resources. Technology will be essential to this but not the top down models that were imposed at massive cost under the New Labour years. We need to start from an understanding of who we are as human beings, what we need and what the realities are of living with each other on this one planet.

We return to our elaboration of the ethic of care from Chapter Two. We are entangled with each other, needing and giving care at all sorts of points in the life cycle. Care of the self and others are meaningful activities in their own right, involving everyone – men and women, old and young, able bodied and disabled. In giving and receiving care, everyone can, in the right conditions of mutual respect and material support, learn the civic responsibilities of responsibility, trust, tolerance for human limitation and frailties, and acceptance of diversity. Care as an organising concept for social work requires that we reconnect with the core values of social work, usefully summarised in the definition of social work provided by the International Federation of Social Workers:

> The social work profession promotes social change, problem solving in human relationships and the empowerment and liberation of people to enhance well-being. Utilising theories of human behaviour and social systems, social work intervenes at the points where people interact with their environments. Principles of human rights and social justice are fundamental to social work.

Replacing risk with care opens up new opportunities for engaging with community and family practices, for situating services within a different paradigm and has the potential to infuse policy, law and the configuration of services as we seek to build not break relationships. Care enables social work to conceptualise and develop ethical practice in fresh ways. Using care as an organising principle encourages practice and provision to consider capacities and strengths, but does not imply that social work only encounters care full relationships. We have examined the turbulence and harm children, families and communities encounter or generate. But, if we maintain risk as the paradigm within which we practise and understand the lives we seek to change, then our work will be limited and unsafe.

Care as a guiding principle would expect social work to be concerned with the context in which families lived, that lived experiences mattered in addressing change. As Barnes (2012) argues, care is not – as often portrayed – at odds with social justice, but is a conceptual framework that enables social work to take seriously social and economic inequalities in the building of care full practice with vulnerable children and families. We have offered examples in the book of careful practices.

> Members of the Participle team lived alongside a number of families that our Swindon partners identified as most problematic, staying in empty council accommodation on some of the estates. Eight weeks were spent experiencing the lived reality of the families' lives: doing the school run, shopping on the high street, spending social evenings in the local pub, searching for their children after dark and witnessing negotiations with loan sharks. We also gave families cameras to film things 'we wouldn't know about them' and discovered family members who were keen

horse riders, actors, maths whizzes, novel writers and artists. Finally, we sat on their sofas as a succession of policemen, social workers, learning support officers, housing officers and others made their calls. (Cottam, 2013: 9)

Seed and champion alternative models

We have seen a range of attempts to develop alternative models as we have indicated. Indeed, Lonne et al (2009) offer a sustained discussion including exploring those such as Differential Response Models where attempts are made to develop system responses that are flexible and not risk saturated. We have seen models develop within local authorities such as Reclaiming Social Work in Hackney (Goodman and Trowler, 2011) and, indeed, we sense a hunger for alternate models as evidenced by the interest in local authorities in rolling out differing approaches. We have also noted the importance of learning from our history in social work.

We have argued in this book for the importance of learning from those models not focused explicitly on child protection such as the work of Participle and the Life Programme in Swindon and the New York City parent-led Child Welfare Organizing Project (Tobis, 2013).

We hope that a key aspect of our contribution to these developments is the importance we attach to interrogating the ethics of what we do in an unequal society and not losing this in a focus on what is done. Addressing why, how and what questions seems to us imperative.

We also emphasise the importance of being modest about what is knowable and what is not, since a great deal of resource is spent serving the pretence of certainty. The rise of deterministic agendas concerned with 'what works' can close off rather than open up innovatory possibilities. Our capacity to help is strengthened by understanding there may be a range of options and that there may also be possibilities that emerge from the dialogue we engage in and the dynamic nature of family experiences. We welcome the challenges that arise from trying to build practice responses that bridge the domains of tested programmes, responsivity and uncertainty.

Facilitate the dialogue

In Chapters Six, Seven and Eight we argued for new forms of conversation between families: conversations that explored dreams, hopes, meanings, fears, loves, and desires. Such conversations need to run through our society. Cottam (2013) emphasises that, through new conversations, something shared, collective and relational will be grown. As academic researchers, parents, foster parents, former social workers and citizens we have written this book in order to support such dialogue.

Concluding thoughts

This has been a book concerned with social work and social workers, not because we think they are the only professionals that matter, or indeed should matter, in the tasks of supporting families. But because it is where we come from and dominant practices concern us greatly. At the time of writing we note the emergence of initiatives such as Frontline designed to deliver new leaders for social work in the task of 'child protection'. What we propose for our profession might also be seen as a form of leadership – but it is a humble and humane vision of leadership in the service of working to ensure that children can be cared for safely, as far as possible, within families that are supported to flourish economically and socially, and encouraged to be and do the very best they can.

References

Aldgate, J. and Tunstill, J. (2000) *Services for children in need: From policy to practice*, London: Stationery Office.

Allen, G. (2011a) *Early intervention: The next steps*, An Independent Report to Her Majesty's Government, London: HMSO.

Allen, G. (2011b) *Early intervention: Smart investments, massive savings*, An Independent Report to Her Majesty's Government, London: HMSO.

Argyris, C. (1999) *On organisational learning*, Oxford: Oxford University Press.

Ashley, C., Featherstone, B., Roskill, C., Ryan, M. and White, S. (2006) *Fathers matter*, London: Family Rights Group.

Ashby, W. R. (1956) *An introduction to cybernetics*, London: Chapman & Hall.

Axford, N. (2010) 'Is social exclusion a useful concept in children's services?', *British Journal of Social Work*, vol 40, no 3, pp 737–54.

Baker, D., Gustafson, S., Beaubien, J., Salas, E., and Barach, P. (2005), *Medical teamwork and patient safety: The evidence-based relation*, Rockville, MD: Agency for Healthcare Research and Quality.

Banks, S. (1995) *Ethics and values in social work*, London: BASW/Macmillan.

Barlow, J., Fisher, J. D. and Jones, D. (2012) *Systematic review of models of analysing significant harm*, Department for Education, London: The Stationery Office.

Barnes, M. (2008) 'Deliberating with care: Ethics and knowledge in the making of social policies', Inaugural Lecture, University of Brighton.

Barnes, M. (2012) *Care in everyday life: An ethic of care in practice*, Bristol: Policy Press.

Batchelor, J. (2003) 'Working with family change; repartnering and stepfamily life', in M. Bell and K. Wilson (eds) *The practitioner's guide to working with families*, Basingstoke: Palgrave/Macmillan.Barclay, P. M. (1982) *Social workers: Their roles and tasks*, London, Bedford: Square Press.

Bebbington, A. and Miles, J. (1989) 'The background of children who enter local authority care', *British Journal of Social Work*, vol 19, no 5, pp 349–68.

Beck, U. and Beck-Gernsheim, E. (1995) *The normal chaos of love*, Cambridge: Polity.

Beck, U. and Beck-Gernsheim, E. (2002) *Individualization*, London: Sage.

Becker, S. and MacPherson, S. (1988) *Public issues, private pain: Poverty, social work and social policy*, London: Social Services Insight Books.

Belsky, J. and de Haan, M. (2011) 'Parenting and children's brain development: the end of the beginning', *Journal of Child Psychology and Psychiatry*, vol 52, no 4, pp 409–28.

Bernstein, R. J. (1983) *Beyond objectivism and relativism: Science hermeneutics and praxis,* Philadelphia: University of Pennsylvania Press.

Best, J. (1990) *Threatened children: Rhetoric and concern about child-victims,* Chicago: University of Chicago Press.

Bevan, G. and Hood, C. (2006) 'What's measured is what matters: Targets and gaming in the English public health care system', *Public Administration*, vol 84, no 3, pp 517–38.

Biestek, F. (1957) *The casework relationship,* Chicago, IL: Loyola University Press.

Blewett, J. and Tunstill, J. (2013) 'Mapping the journey: outcome-focused practice and the role of interim outcomes in family support services', *Child and Family Social Work,* doi: 10.1111/cfs.12073.

Blond, P. (2010) *Red Tory: How Left and Right have broken Britain and how we can fix it,* London: Faber.

Bourdieu, P. (1999) *The weight of the world: Social Suffering in contemporary society,* Cambridge: Polity.

Broadhurst, K., Wastell, D., White, S., Hall, C., Peckover, S., Thompson, K., Pithouse, A. and Davey, D. (2009) 'Performing 'initial assessment': identifying the latent conditions for error at the front-door of local authority children's services', *British Journal of Social Work Advance Access*, vol 1, no 19.

Brown, R. H. (1994) 'Reconstructing social theory after the postmodern critique', in H. W. Simons and M. Billig (eds) *After postmodernism: Reconstructing ideology critique*, London: Sage.

Brown, R. and Ward, H. (2013) *Decision-making within the child's timeframe,* London: DfE.

Bruer, J. T. (1999) *The myth of the first three years,* New York: The Free Press.

Burkitt, I. (2008) *Social selves* (2nd edn), London: Sage.

Butler, J. (2004) *Precarious life: The powers of mourning and violence,* London: Verso.

Butler, J. (2005) *Giving an account of oneself,* New York: Fordham University Press.

Bywaters, P. (forthcoming) 'Inequalities in child welfare: Towards a new policy, research and action agenda', *British Journal of Social Work*.

Butler-Sloss, E. (1988) *Report of the inquiry into child abuse in Cleveland 1987,* London: Her Majesty's Stationery Office.

CAFCASS (2012) *Three weeks in November... three years on...* CAFCASS care application study 2012, www.cafcass.gov.uk.

Cartwright, N. and Munro, E. (2010) 'The limitations of randomized controlled trials in predicting effectiveness', *Journal of Evaluation in Clinical Practice*, vol 16, no 2, pp 260–6.

Casey, L. (2012) *Listening to troubled families*, London: Troubled Families Unit.

CCETSW (1991) *DipSW: Rules and requirements for the Diploma in Social Work, Paper 30*, London: Central Council for Education and Training in Social Work.

Chan, Y. E. and Reich, B. H. (2007) 'IT alignment: what have we learned?'. *Journal of Information technology*, vol 22, no 4, pp 297–315.

Chesterton, G. G. K and Perry, M. W. (2000) *Eugenics and other evils: An argument against the Scientifically organized state*, Oxford: Inkling Books.

Chief Secretary to the Treasury (2003) *Every Child Matters* Cmnd 5860. The Stationery Office: London.

Choudry, S., Herring, J. and Wallbank, J. (2010) 'Welfare, rights, care and gender in family law' in J. Wallbank, J. S. Choudry, and J. Herring (eds) *Rights, gender and family law*, London: Routledge.

Churchill, H. (2012) 'The retreating state? Recent developments in family support policies' in M. Kilkey, G. Ramia and K. Farnsworth (eds) *Social policy review 24: Analysis and debate in social policy 2012*, Bristol: The Policy Press.

Churchill, H. and Clarke, K. (2009) 'Investing in parent education: A critical review of policy and provision under New Labour', *Social Policy and Society*, vol 9, no 1, pp 39–53.

Connell, R. W. (1995) *Masculinities*, Cambridge: Polity.

Cooper, J. and Vetere, A. (2005) *Domestic violence and family safety*, London: Whurr Publishers Ltd.

Cottam, H. (2011) 'Relational welfare', *Soundings,* vol 48, pp 134–44.

Cottam, H. (2013) *The Life Programme: An interim report*, London: Participle, www.alifewewant.com.

Coulter, M. (2013) 'Strength to change', paper presented at Safeguarding and Domestic Violence Conference, Durham, 21 May 2013.

Crichton, N. (2012) Keynote address, BAPSCAN, Queen's University Belfast, 17 April.

Cross, R. and Borgatti, S. P. (2004) 'The ties that share: Relational characteristics that facilitate information seeking', in M. Huysman, and V. Wulf (eds) *Social capital and information technology*, Boston: MIT, pp 137–59.

Culpitt, I. (1999) *Social policy and risk*, London: Sage.

Dale, P., Davies, M., Morrison, T. and Waters, J. (1986) *Dangerous families: Assessment and treatment of child abuse*, London: Tavistock.

Davies, H. and Mannion, R. (2013) 'Will prescriptions for cultural change improve the NHS?' *BMJ*, 1 March 2013.

Dekker, S. (2007) *Just culture balancing safety and accountability*, Aldershot: Ashgate Publishing Company.

de Montigny, G. (1995) *Social working: An ethnography of front line practice*, Toronto: University of Toronto Press.

De Sitter, L. U., Den Hertog, J. F., and Dankbaarl, B. (1997) 'From complex organizations with simple jobs to simple organizations with complex jobs', *Human Relations*, vol 50, no 5, pp 497–534.

Denney, D. (1996) 'Discrimination and anti-discrimination in probation' in T. May and A. Vass (eds) *Working with offenders: Issues, contexts and outcomes*, London: Sage.

Department for Education (2010) Haringey Safeguarding Children Board, Serious Case Review 'Child A' http://media.education.gov. uk/assets/files/pdf/s/second%20serious%20case%20overview%20 report%20relating%20to%20peter%20connelly%20dated%20 march%202009.pdf

Department for Education (DfE) (2013) *Working together to safeguard children*, London: The Stationery Office.

Department of Health (1995) *Child protection: Messages from research*, London: The Stationery Office.

Dermott, E. (2008) *Intimate fatherhood*, London: Routledge.

Dermott, E., Gabb, J. and Featherstone, B. (2013) 'Fragile fathers', presented at International Conference on Families and Relationships, Centre for Research on Families and Relationships, Edinburgh, 10–12 June 2013.

Dickens, J., Howell, D., Thoburn, J. and Schofield, G. (2007) 'Children starting to be looked after by local authorities in England: an analysis of inter-authority variation and case-centred decision making', *British Journal of Social Work*, vol 37, no 4, pp 597–617.

Dingwall, R., Eekelaar, J. and Murray, T. (1983) *The protection of children: State intervention and family life*, Oxford: Blackwell.

Dolan, P., Canavan, J. and Pinkerton, J. (eds) (2006) *Family support as reflective practice*, London: Jessica Kingsley.

Doolan, M. (2007) 'Duty Calls: The response of law, policy and practice to participation right in child welfare systems', *Protecting Children*, vol 22, no 1, pp 10–18.

Edwards, A., Barnes, M. and Plewis, I. (2006) *Working to prevent the social exclusion of children and young people: Final lessons from the national evaluation of the Children's Fund*, London: Department for Education and Schools Research, Report 734.

Eraut, M. (1994) *Developing professional knowledge and competence*, Abingdon: Routledge Falmer.

Evans, R., Pinnock, K., Beirens, H. and Edwards, A. (2006) *Developing preventative practices: The experiences of children and families*, London: Department for Education and Schools Research Report 735.

Fawcett, B., Featherstone, B. and Goddard, J. (2004) *Contemporary child care policy and practice*, Basingstoke: Palgrave Macmillan.

Featherstone, B. (1999) 'Taking mothering seriously: The implications for child protection', *Child and Family Social Work*, vol 4, no 1, pp 43–55.

Featherstone, B. (2004a) *Family life and family support: A feminist analysis*, Basingstoke: Palgrave Macmillan.

Featherstone, B. (2004b) 'Feminist social work: Past, present and future' in S. Hick, J. Fook and R. Pozutto (eds) *Social work: A critical turn*, Canada: Thompson Education Press.

Featherstone, B. (2009) *Contemporary fathering: Theory, policy and practice*, Bristol: The Policy Press.

Featherstone, B. (2010) 'Writing fathers in but mothers out!!!', *Critical Social Policy*, vol 30, no 2, pp 208–24.

Featherstone, B. (2013) 'Working with fathers: risk or resource' in J. Ribbens McCarthy, C-A. Hooper and V. Gillies, (eds) *Family Troubles: Exploring changes and challenges in the family lives of children and young people*, Bristol: Policy Press.

Featherstone, B. and Fraser, C. (2009) *Parents' views of services*, Bradford: Bradford Metropolitan District Council.

Featherstone, B. and Fraser, C. (2012a) '"I'm just a mother: they're all professionals": Advocacy for parents as an aid to parental engagement', *Child and Family Social Work*, vol 17, no 2, pp 244–53.

Featherstone, B. and Fraser, C. (2012b) 'Working with fathers and domestic violence: Contemporary debates', *Child Abuse Review*, vol 21, pp 255–63.

Featherstone, B. and Lancaster, E. (1997) 'Contemplating the unthinkable: Men who sexually abuse', *Critical Social Policy*, vol 17, no 4, pp 51–73.

Featherstone, B. and Morris, K. (2012) 'The feminist ethics of care' in M. Gray, J. Midgley and S. Webb (eds) *The SAGE handbook of social work*, London: Sage.

Featherstone, B. and White, S. (2006) 'Fathers talk about their lives and services' in C. Ashley B. Featherstone, C. Roskill, M. Ryan and S. White (eds), *Fathers matter*, London: Family Rights Group.

Featherstone, B., Broadhurst, K. and Holt, K. (2012) 'Thinking systemically – thinking politically, building strong relationships with children and families in a context of rising inequality', *British Journal of Social Work*, vol 42, pp 618–33.

Featherstone, B., Manby, M. and Nicholls, N. (2007) 'What difference does outreach make to family support?' in J. Schneider, M. Avis and P. Leighton (eds) *Supporting children and families: Lessons from Sure Start for evidence-based practice in health, social care and education*, London: Jessica Kingsley Publishers.

Featherstone, B., Morris, K. and White, S. (2013) 'A marriage made in hell: Early intervention meets child protection', *British Journal of Social Work*, doi: 10.1093/bjsw/bct052.

Featherstone, B., Rivett, M. and Scourfield, J. (2007) *Working with men in health and social care*, London: Sage.

Featherstone, B., White, S. and Wastell, D. (2012) 'Ireland's opportunity to learn from England's difficulties? Auditing uncertainty in child protection', *Irish Journal of Applied Social Studies*, vol 12, no 1, pp 28–42

Featherstone, B., Fraser C., Ashley, C. and Ledward, P. (2011) 'Advocacy for parents and carers involved with children's services: Making a difference to working in partnership?' *Child and Family Social Work*, vol 16, no 3, pp 266–75.

Featherstone, B., Fraser, C., O'Dell, L., Pritchard, D. and Tarrant, A. (2012) 'An evaluation of Family Rights Group advice and advocacy services', www.frg.org.uk.

Ferguson, H. (2001) 'Promoting, child protection, welfare and healing', *Child and Family Social Work*, vol 6, no 1, pp 1–13.

Ferguson, H. and Hogan, F. (2004) *Strengthening families thorough fathers*, Dublin: Family Support Agency.

Feyerabend, P. (2001), *Conquest of abundance: A tale of abstraction versus the richness of being*, Chicago: University of Chicago Press.

Finch, J. (2007) 'Displaying families', *Sociology*, vol 41, pp 65–81.

Flax, J. (1990) *Thinking fragments: Psychoanalysis, feminism and postmodernism in the contemporary west*, Berkeley, CA: University of California Press.

Fleck, L. (1979) *Genesis and development of scientific fact*, Chicago: University of Chicago Press.

Fletcher, R. (1966) *The family and marriage in Britain*, Harmondsworth: Penguin.

Forrester, D., McCambridge, J., Waissbein, C. and Rollnick, S. (2007) 'How do child and family social workers talk to parents about child protection issues?', *Child Abuse Review*, vol 17, pp 23–35.

Forrester, D. (2012) 'Evaluation Research' in M. Gray; J. Midgley and S. A. Webb (Eds), *The SAGE Handbook of Social Work*, London: Sage pp440-453.

Fox Harding, L. (1997) *Perspectives in child care policy* (2nd edn), Essex: Longman.

Fox Harding, L. (1999) '"Family values" and Conservative government policy' in G. Jagger and C. Wright (eds) *Changing family values*, London: Routledge.

Fowler, B. (2009) 'The recognition/redistribution debate and Bourdieu's theory of practice', *Theory, Culture and Society*, vol 26, no 1, pp 144–56.

Fraser, N. (1997) *Justice interruptus: Critical reflections on the 'postsocialist' condition*, New York: Routledge.

Fraser, N. (2000) 'Rethinking recognition', *New Left Review*, vol 3, pp 107–20.

Frost, P. and Hoggett, P. (2008) 'Human agency and social suffering', *Critical Social Policy*, vol 28, no 4, pp 438–60.

Frost, N. and Parton, N. (2009) *Understanding children's social care: Politics, policy and practice*, London: Sage.

Gadd, D. (2004) 'Evidence led or policy led evidence: Cognitive behavioural programmes for men who are violent towards women', *Criminal Justice*, vol 4, pp 173–97.

GAIN Working Group E, Flight Ops/ATC Ops Safety Information Sharing (2004) *A road map to a just culture,* www.flightsafety.org.

Gambrill, E. (2012) *Propaganda in the helping professions*, Oxford: Oxford University Press.

Gardner, R. (2002) *Supporting families: Child protection in the community*, Chichester: Wiley.

Gesell, A. and Ilg, F. L. (1943) *Infant and child in the culture of today. The guidance of development in home and nursery school*, New York: Harper and Brothers.

Ghate, D. and Hazel, N. (2002) *Parenting in poor environments: Stress, support and coping*, London: Jessica Kingsley Publishers.

Gibson, J. and O'Donovan, B. (2012) 'A systems approach to the design and management of English and Welsh Children's Services departments', Lean in Public Services and Higher Education: Transforming the Public Sector Conference, Portsmouth.

Gibson, M. (2013) 'Shame and guilt in child protection social work: new interpretations and opportunities for practice', *Child & Family Social Work*, doi: 10.1111/cfs.12081.

Giddens, A. (1992) *The transformation of intimacy*, Cambridge: Polity.

Giddens, A. (1998) *The third way: The renewal of social democracy*, Cambridge: Polity.

Gilbert, N. (1997) (ed) *Combatting child abuse: International perspectives and trends*, New York: Oxford University Press.

Gilbert, N., Parton, N. and Skiveness, M. (2011) 'Changing patterns of responses and emerging orientations' in N. Gilbert, N. Parton and M. Skiveness (eds) *Child protection systems: International trends and orientations*, Oxford: Oxford University Press.

Gillies, V. (2005) 'Meeting parents' needs? Discourses of "support" and "inclusion" in family policy', *Critical Social Policy*, vol 25, no 1, pp 70–90.

Gillies, V. (2007) *Marginalised mothers: Exploring working class experiences of parenting*, Abingdon: Routledge.

Gilligan, C. (1983) *In a different voice*, Cambridge, MA: Harvard University Press.

Goffman, E. (1968) *Stigma: Notes on the management of spoiled identity*, Harmondsworth: Pelican.

Goldner, V., Penn, P., Sheinberg, M. and Walker, G. (1990) 'Love and violence: gender paradoxes in volatile attachments', *Family Process*, vol 29, no 4, pp 343–64.

Gondolf, E. (2002) *Batterer intervention systems*, Thousand Oaks: Sage.

Goodman, S. and Trowler, I. (2011) *Social work reclaimed: Innovative frameworks for child and family social work practice*, London: Jessica Kingsley Publishers.

Gray, M. and Webb, S.A. (eds) (2010) *Ethics and value perspectives in social work*. Basingstoke: Palgrave.

Greenhalgh, T. and Russell, J. (2006) 'Reframing evidence synthesis as rhetorical action in the policy-making drama', *Healthcare Policy*, vol 1, no 2, pp 34–42.

Hacking, I. (1999) *The social construction of what?*, London: Harvard University Press.

Haidt, J. (2001) 'The emotional dog and its rational tail: a social intuitionist approach to moral judgement', *Psychological Review*, vol 108, no 4, pp 814–34.

Hall, C., Parton, N., Peckover, S. and White, S. (2010) 'Child-centric ICTs and the fragmentation of child welfare practice in England', *Journal of Social Policy*, vol 39, no 3, pp 393–413.

Hall, S. (2011) 'The neoliberal revolution', *Soundings*, vol 48, pp 9–27.

Hardham, V. (2006) 'Bridges to safe uncertainty: An interview with Barry Mason', *Australia and New Zealand Journal of Family Therapy*, vol 27, no 1, pp 16–21.

Harris, N. and Gosnell, L. (2012) *From the perspective of parents: Interviews following a child protection investigation*, Canberra: Australian National University.

Harvey, D. (2005) *A short history of neoliberalism*, Oxford: Oxford University Press.

Hekman, S. (1995) *Moral voices, moral selves: Carol Gilligan and feminist moral theory*, Cambridge: Polity Press.

Herzberg, F., Mausner, B., and Snyderman, B. B. (1959) *The motivation to work*, New York: John Wiley & Sons.

Hey, V (2001) 'Troubling the auto/biography of the questions: re/thinking rapport and the politics of social class in feminist observations', *Studies in Educational Ethnography*, vol 3, pp 161–83.

Hicks, S. (2008) 'Gender role models... who needs 'em?', *Qualitative Social Work*, vol 7, no 1.

Holland, S., Tunnock, S. and Evans, R. (2011) *Safeguarding children and young people in local communities: A WISERD local knowledge in context project*, Wales: Wales Institute of Social and Economic Research, Data and Methods.

Holman, B. (2013) 'The case for preventive community work is returning', *The Guardian*, 16 October.

Home Office (1998) *Supporting families: A consultation document*, London: Home Office.

Honneth, A. (1995) *The struggle for recognition: The moral grammar of social conflicts*, Cambridge: Polity Press.

Hood, R. (2012a) 'A critical realist model of complexity for interprofessional working', *Journal of Interprofessional Care*, vol 26, no 1.

Hood, R. (2012b) 'Complexity and integrated working in children's services', *British Journal of Social Work*, doi: 10.1093/bjsw/bcs091.

Hooper, C-A., Gorin, S., Cabral, C. and Dyson, C. (2007) *Living with hardship 24/7: The diverse experiences of families in poverty in England*, London: The Frank Buttle Trust.

Howe, D. (1996) 'Surface and depth in social work practice' in N. Parton (ed) *Social theory, social change and social work*, London: Routledge.

Howe, D., Brandon, M., Hinings, D. and Schofield, G. (1999) *Attachment theory, child maltreatment and family support*, Basingstoke: Palgrave Macmillan.

Houston, S. (2010) 'Discourse ethics' in M. Gray and S. A. Webb (eds) *Ethics and value perspectives in social work*, Basingstoke: Palgrave.

Hudson J. (2002) 'Digitising the structure of government: the UK's information age government agenda', *Policy and Politics*, 30: 515–31.

Hughes, N. and Fielding, T. (2006) *Targeting preventative services: Experiences from the Children's Fund*, London: DfE Research Report RR777.

Hugman, R. and Smith, D. (1995) 'Ethical issues in social work: an overview' in R. Hugman and D. Smith (eds) *Ethical issues in social work*, London: Routledge.

Hunt, J., Waterhouse, S. and Lutman, E. (2008) *Keeping them in the family: Children placed in kinship care through care proceedings*, London: BAAF.

Hyde, L. (1998) *Trickster makes this world: Mischief, myth and art*, North Point Press: New York.

Ivec, M., Braithwaite, V. and Harris, N. (2011) 'Resettling the relationship in indigenous child protection: Public hope and private reality', *Law and Policy*, vol 3, no 1.

Jack, G. (2010) 'Place matters: The significance of place attachments for children's well-being', *British Journal of Social Work*, vol 40, pp 755–71.

Jack, G. and Gill, O. (2010) 'The Role of communities in safeguarding children and young people', *Child Abuse Review*, vol 19, pp 82–96.

Jamieson, L. (1998) *Intimacy: Personal relationships in modern society*, Cambridge: Polity.

Jenson, J. and Saint-Martin, D. (2001) 'Changing citizenship regimes: Social policy strategies in the social investment state', workshop on 'Fostering social cohesion: A comparison of new policy strategies', Universite de Montreal, 21–22 June 2001.

Johnson, M. (1995) 'Patriarchal terrorism and common couple violence: two forms of violence against women', *Journal of Marriage and the Family*, vol 57, pp 43–59 and 283–94.

Jordan, B. (1991) 'Competencies and values', *Social Work Education*, vol 10, no 1.

Jordan, B. and Drakeford, M. (2012) *Social work and social policy under austerity*, Basingstoke: Palgrave Macmillan.

Jordan, B. and Jordan, C. (2000) *Social work and the third way: Tough love as social policy*, London: Sage.

Judt, T. (2010) *Ill fares the land*, London: Penguin.

Kahneman, D., Sloveic, P. and Tversky, A. (1982) *Judgement under uncertainty: Heuristics and biases*. New York: Cambridge University Press.

Kemp, S. O., Marcenko, M., Hoagwood, K. and Vesneski, W. (2004) 'Engaging parents in child welfare services: Bridging family needs and child welfare mandates', *Child Welfare*, vol 88, no 1, pp 101–26.

Knorr-Cetina, K. and Mulkay, M. (1983) 'Introduction: emerging principles in the social study of science' in K. Knorr-Cetina and M. Mulkay (eds) *Science observed: Perspectives on the social study of science*, Beverley Hills, CA: Sage

Kemshall, H. (2002) *Risk, social policy and welfare*, Buckingham: Open University Press.

Kirton, D. (2013) '"Kinship by design" in England: reconfiguring adoption from Blair to the coalition', *Child and Family Social Work*, vol 18, pp 97–106.

Kleinman, A. and Kleinman, J. (1991) 'Suffering and its professional transformation: towards an ethnography of interpersonal experience', *Culture, Medicine and Psychiatry*, vol 15, no 3, pp 275–301.

Krumer-Nevo, M. (2003) 'From "a coalition of despair" to "a covenant of help" in social work with families in distress', *European Journal of Social Work*, vol 6, no 3, pp 273–82.

Latour, B. (1999) *Pandora's hope: Essays on the reality of science studies*, London: Harvard University Press.

Laming, H. (2003) *The Victoria Climbié Inquiry: Report of an Inquiry by Lord Laming*, The Stationery Office: Norwich.

Levine, M. and Levine, A. (2002) 'Neighbourhood-based services: Lessons from the Settlement House Movement and the war on poverty' in G. Melton, R. Thompson, and M. Small (eds) *Towards a child-centered, neigbourhood-based child protection system: A report of the Consortium on Children, Families, and the Law*, Westport CT: Praeger.

Levitas, R. (2005) *The inclusive society? Social exclusion and New Labour*, Basingstoke: Palgrave.

Levitas, R. (2012a) 'The just's umbrella: austerity and the Big Society in coalition policy and beyond', *Critical Social Policy*, vol 32, no 3, pp 320–42.

Levitas, R. (2012b) Policy Response Series No.3, *There may be 'trouble' ahead: what we know about those 120,000 'troubled' families*, PSE UK www.poverty.ac.uk/policy-response, accessed December 2012.

Lillrank, P. and Liukko, M. (2004) 'Standard, routine and non-routine processes in health care', *International Journal of Health Care Quality Assurance*, vol 17, no 1, pp 39–46.

Lindley, B. and Richards, M. (2002) *Protocol on advice and advocacy for parents (Child protection)*, Centre for Family Research: Cambridge.

Lister, R. (2004) *Poverty: Key concepts*, Cambridge: Polity.

Lister, R. (2006) 'An agenda for children: investing in the future or promoting well-being in the present?' in J. Lewis (ed) *Children, changing families and welfare states*, Edward Elgar: Cheltenham.

Little, M. (1995) *Humane medicine*, Cambridge: Cambridge University Press.

Little, M. and Axford, N. (2004) *Refocusing children's services: Lessons from the literature*, London: Department for Education and Skills.

Lonne, B., Parton, N., Thomson, J. and Harries, M. (2009) *Reforming child protection*, London: Routledge.

Loveless, L. (2012) 'Weighing up the evidence: implementing joint commissioning in children's services', Unpublished PhD Thesis, University of Birmingham.

McCrory, E., De Brito, S. and Viding, E. (2012) 'The link between child abuse andpsychopathology: a review of neurobiological and genetic research', *Journal of theRoyal Society of Medicine*, 105: 151–6.

McNay, L, (2008) 'The trouble with recognition: Subjectivity, suffering and agency', *Sociological Theory*, vol 26, no 3, pp 271–96.

McQueen, P. (2011) 'Social and political recognition', Internet Encyclopedia of Philosophy, www.iep.utm.edu.

MacIntyre, A. (2007) *After virtue* (3rd edn), Notre Dame, IN: University of Notre Dame Press.

Mahadevan, J. (2012) 'BBC social work film prompts calls for early police support', Children and Young People Now, www.cypnow.co.uk.

Mannion, R., Konteh, F. and Davies, H. (2009) 'Assessing organisational culture for quality and safety improvement: a national survey of tools and tool use', *Quality and Safety in Health Care*, vol 18, pp 153–6.

Margolin, L. (1997) *Under the cover of kindness: The invention of social work*, Virginia: University Press of Virginia.

Mason, B. (2005) 'Relational risk-taking and the training of supervisors', *Journal of Family Therapy*, vol 27, pp 298–301.

Mason, P. and Prior, D. (2008) *Engaging young people who offend*, Youth Justice Board, www.yjb.gov.uk.

Masson, J. and Dickens, J. (2013) *Partnership by Law? The Pre-proceedings process for families on the edge of care proceedings*, Report of ESRC RES-062-2226.

Meadows, P. (2011) *National evaluation of Sure Start local programmes: An economic perspective*, DfE Research Report DFE-RR073, London: Department for Education.

Melton, G. (2009) 'Preface' in B. Lonne, N. Parton, J.

Thomson and M. Harries (2009) *Reforming child protection*, London: Routledge.

Melton, G., Thompson, R. A. and Small, M. A. (2002) (eds) *Towards a child-centered, neighbourhood-based child protection system: A report of the Consortium on Children, Families, and the Law*, Westport, CT: Praeger.

Morgan, D. (1996) *Family connections*, Cambridge: Polity Press.

Moore, S. (2012) 'Now instead of being disgusted by poverty, we are disgusted by poor people themselves', *The Guardian*, 16 February.

Morris, K. (2005) 'From 'children in need' to 'children at risk' – Mapping the policy changes in children's preventative services', *Practice*, vol 17, no 12, pp 67–79.

Morris, K. (2011) 'Family support: Policies for practice' in M. Davis (ed) *Social Work with children and families,* Basingstoke: Palgrave MacMillan.

Morris, K. (2012) 'Troubled families: Their experiences of using multiple services', Nottingham City Council (unpublished).

Morris, K. and Burford, G. (2009) 'Family decision making: New spaces for resistance and participation' in M. Barnes and D. Prior (eds) *Subversive citizens,* Bristol: Policy Press.

Morris, K. and Featherstone, B. (2010) 'Investing in children, regulating parents and supporting whole families', *Social Policy and Society,* vol 9, no 4, pp 557–86.

Morris, K., Brandon, M. and Tudor, P. (2012) *Family involvement in serious case reviews,* York: BASPCAN.

Morris, K. Brandon, M. and Tudor, P. (2013) 'Rights, responsibilities and pragmatic practice', *Child Abuse Review,* Published online in Wiley Online Library (wileyonlinelibrary.com), DOI: 10.1002/car.2272

Morris, K., Hughes, N., Clarke, H., Tew, J., Mason, P., Galvani, S., Lewis, A., Loveless, L., Becker, S. and Burford, G. (2009) *Think family: A literature review of whole family approaches,* London: Cabinet Office.

Munro, E. (2011) *The Munro Review of child protection: Final report – A child-centred system,* London: Department for Education.

Murray, L. and Barnes, M. (2010) 'Have *families* been rethought? Ethic of care, *family* and "whole" *family* approaches', *Social Policy and Society,* vol 9, no 4.

National Patient Safety Agency (2011) *Patient safety first. The campaign review,* London: National Patient Safety Agency.

Nussbaum, M. (1997) *Cultivating humanity: A classical defense of reform in liberal education,* Cambridge, MA: Harvard University Press.

OECD (2011) 'Growing income inequality in OECD countries: what drives it and how can policy tackle it?', OECD Forum on Tacking Inequality, Paris, 2 May 2011.

Ofsted (2012) 'Inspection of local authority arrangements for the protection of children', Birmingham City Council, www.ofsted. gov.uk.

Oldridge, D. (2007) *Strange histories: The trial of the pig, the walking dead and other matters of fact from the medieval and renaissance worlds,* Abingdon: Routledge.

Oliver, C., Owen, C., Statham, J. and Moss, P. (2001) *Facts and figures: Local authority variance on indicators concerning child protection and children looked after,* London: Thomas Coram Research Unit.

Orme, J. (2001) *Gender and community care: Social work and social care perspectives,* Basingstoke: Palgrave Macmillan.

Orme, J. (2002) 'Social work: Gender, care and justice', *British Journal of Social Work*, vol 32, pp 799–814.

Parton, N (1991) *Governing the family, child care, child protection and the state*, Basingstoke: Palgrave Macmillan.

Parton, N. (2003) 'Rethinking professional practice: the contribution of social constructivism and feminist ethic of care', *British Journal of Social Work*, vol 33, no 1, pp 1–16.

Patterson, C (2012) 'A second chance for a bad parent can mean a life sentence for a child', *The Independent*, 11 February 2012.

Pence, E. and Paymar, M. (1993) *Education groups for men who batter*, New York: Springer.

Plato (2007) *The republic*, London: Penguin Classics.

Platt, D., & Turney, D. (2013) 'Making threshold decisions in child protection: a conceptual analysis.' *British Journal of Social Work*. Advance Access doi: *10.1093/bjsw/bct007*

Power, A. (2007) *City survivors: Bringing up children in disadvantaged neighbourhoods*, Bristol: Policy Press.

Radford, D. (2013) 'NSCC project working with mothers and children in the context of domestic abuse', Paper presented at Domestic Violence and Safeguarding conference, Durham, 21 May.

Reason, J. (1997) *Managing the risks of organizational accidents*, Aldershot: Ashgate.

Reason, J. (2000) 'Human error: Models and management', *British Medical Journal*, vol 320, pp 768–70.

Reder, P. and Duncan, S. (2003) 'Understanding communication in child protection networks', *Child Abuse Review*, vol 12, pp 82–100.

Reid, W. J. and Shyne, A. W. (1969). *Brief and extended casework*, Columbia: University Press.

Respect (2010) Respect UK statement on 'Caring Dads' programme, www.respect.net.

Revans, L. (2009) 'Lurking in the shadows', *Community Care*, vol 9, pp 18–21.

Ribbens McCarthy, J. (2013) 'What is at stake in family troubles? Existential issues and value frameworks' in J. Ribbens McCarthy, C-A. Hooper, and V. Gillies (eds) *Family troubles? Exploring changes and challenges in the family lives of children and young people*, Bristol: Policy Press.

Richmond, M. E. (1922) *What is social case work?* New York: Russell Sage Foundation.

Ridge, T. (2009) *Living with poverty: A review of the literature on children's and families' experiences of poverty*, Department for Work and Pensions, Research Report No 594.

Ridge, T (2013) 'We are all in this together'? The hidden costs of poverty, recession and austerity policies on Britain's poorest children, *Children and Society*, vol 27, pp 406–17.

Rivett, M. (2010) 'Working with violent male carers (fathers and step-fathers)' in B. Featherstone, C-A. Hooper, J. Scourfield, and J. Taylor (eds) *Gender and child welfare in society*, Chichester: Wiley.

Rose, H. and Rose, S. (2012) *Genes, cells and brains: The Promethean promises of the new biology*, London: Verso.

Rose, N. (1996) 'Governing "advanced" liberal democracies' in A. Barry, T. Osborne and N. Rose (eds) *Foucault and political reason*, Chicago, University of Chicago Press

Roskill, C., Featherstone, B., Ashley, C. and Haresnape, S. (2008) *Fathers matter 11*, London: Family Rights Group.

Rossiter, A. (2011) 'Unsettled social work: The challenge of Levinas's ethics', *British Journal of Social Work*, vol 41, pp 980–95.

Rustin, M. (2008) 'New Labour and the theory of globalization', *Critical Social Policy*, vol 28, no 3, pp 273–82.

Scheff, T. (1988) 'Shame and conformity: the defense-emotion system', *American Sociological Review*, vol 53, pp 395–406.

Scheff, T. (1997) *Emotions, the social bond, and human reality: Part/Whole analysis*, Cambridge: Cambridge University Press.

Scott, K. and Crooks, C. (2004) 'Effecting change in maltreating fathers', *Clinical Psychology; Science and Practice*, vol 11, pp 95–111.

Scourfield, J. (2003) *Gender and child protection*, Basingstoke: Palgrave Macmillan.

Seddon, J. (2008). *Systems thinking in the public sector*, Axminster: Triarchy Press.

Sen, A. (2005) 'Human rights and capabilities', *Journal of Human Development*, vol 6, no 2, pp 151–66.

Senge, P. M. (1990) *The fifth discipline: The art and practice of the learning organization*, London: Century Business.

Serres, M. (2007) *Parasite*, Minneapolis: University of Minnesota Press.

Shaw, I., Morris, K. and Edwards, A. (2009) 'Technology, practice and researching organizational innovations, or How great expectations in London and Cardiff are dashed in Lowestoft and Cymtyrch', *Journal of Social Work Practice*, vol 23, no 4, pp 383–400.

Shemmings, D. and Shemmings, Y. (2011), *Understanding disorganised attachment: Theory and practice of working with children and families*, London: Jessica Kingsley.

Sheppard, M. (2011) 'Prevention orientation in Children's Centres: A study of centre managers', *British Journal of Social Work*, vol 10.

Shonkoff, J. and Bales, S. N. (2011) 'Science does not speak for itself: Translating child development research for the public and its policymakers', *Child Development*, vol 82, no 1, pp 17–32.

Sidel, R. (1992) *Women and children last: The plight of poor women in affluent America*, New York: Penguin.

Skeggs, B. (2005) 'The making of class and gender through visualizing moral subject formation', *Sociology*, vol 39, no 5, pp 565–82.

Smith, C. (2001) 'Trust and confidence', *British Journal of Social Work*, vol 31, pp 287–305.

Smart, C. (2007) *Personal life*, Cambridge: Polity.

Smart, C. and Neale, B. (1999) *Family fragments?* Cambridge: Polity.

Stanley, N., Austerberry, H., Bilson, A., Farrelly, N., Hussein, S., Larkins, C., Manthorpe, J. and Ridley, J. (2013) 'Turning away from the public sector in children's out-of-home care: An English experiment', *Children and Youth Services Review*, vol 35, pp 33–39.

Stevenson, O. (2013) *Reflections on a life in social work: A personal & professional memoir*, Hinton House: Buckingham.

Stiles, W. B. and Shapiro, D. A. (1989) 'Abuse of the drug metaphor in psychotherapy process-outcome research', *Clinical Psychology Review*, vol 9, pp 521–43.

Stiles, W. B., Shapiro, D. A. and Elliott, R. (1986) 'Are all psychotherapies equivalent?', *American Psychologist*, vol 41, pp 165–80.

Swan, J. and Scarbrough, H. (2001) 'Knowledge management: Concepts and controversies', *Journal of Management Studies*, vol 38, pp 913–21.

Taylor, C. (2004) 'Underpinning knowledge for child care practice: Reconsidering child development theory', *Child and Family Social Work*, vol 9, no 3, pp 225–35.

Taylor, C. and White, S. (2000) *Practising reflexivity in health and welfare: Making knowledge*. Buckingham: Open University Press.

Thagard, P. (2000) *How scientists explain disease*, Princeton: Princeton University Press.

The Care Inquiry (2013) *Making not breaking: Building relationships for our most vulnerable children*, London: The Care Inquiry.

Thoburn, J. (1994) *Family involvement in the child protection process*, London: HMSO.

Thoburn, J., Cooper, N., Brandon, M. and Connolly, S. (2012) 'The place of "think family" approaches in child and family social work: Messages from a process evaluation of an English pathfinder service', *Children and Youth Services Review*, vol 35, no 2.

Thyer, B. A. and Myers, L. L. (2011) 'The quest for evidence-based practice: A view from the United States', *Journal of Social Work*, vol 11, no 1, pp 8–25.

Tobis, D. (2013) *From pariahs to partners: How parents and their allies changed New York City's child welfare system*, Oxford: Oxford University Press.

Toynbee, P. (2003) *Hard work: Life in low-pay Britain*, London: Bloomsbury.

Tronto, J. (1993) *Moral boundaries: A political argument for an ethic of care*, New York: Routledge.

Tronto, J. (2010) 'Creating caring institutions: Politics, plurality and purpose', *Ethics and Social Welfare*, vol 4, no 2, pp 158–71.

Tunstill, J., Meadows, M., Akhurst, S., Allnock, D., Chrysanthou, J., Garbers, C. and Morley, A. (2005) *Implementing Sure Start local programmes: An in-depth study*, London: Department of Children, Schools and Families.

Turney, D. (2012) 'A relationship- based approach to engaging involuntary clients: the contribution of recognition theory', *Child and Family Social Work*, vol 17, no 2, pp 145-159.

UK Parliament (2013) *Children first: The child protection system in England*, Education Committee, www.publications.parliament.uk.

Uttal, W. R. (2011). *Mind and brain: A critical appraisal of cognitive neuroscience*, Cambridge, MA: MIT Press.

Van Ijzendoorn, M. H., Goldberg, S., Kroonenberg, P. M. and Frenkel, O. J. (1992) 'The relative effects of maternal and child problems on the quality of attachment: a meta-analysis of attachment in clinical samples', *Child Development*, vol 63, no 4, pp 840–58.

Ward, H. and Brown, R. (2013) 'Decision-making within a child's timeframe: A response', *Family Law Journal*, vol 43, pp 1181–86.

Wastell, D.G. (1996) 'The fetish of technique: methodology as social defence', *Information Systems Journal*, vol 6, pp 25–40.

Wastell, D. G. (2011) *Managers as designers in the public services: Beyond technomagic*, Devon: Triarchy Press.

Wastell, D. and White, S. (2012) 'Blinded by neuroscience: Social policy, the family and the infant brain', *Families, Relationships and Society*, vol 1, no 3, pp 397–414.

Wastell, D., White, S., Broadhurst, K., Hall, C., Peckover, S. and Pithouse, A. (2010) 'Children's services in the iron cage of performance management: street level bureaucracy and the spectre of Švejkism', *International Journal of Social Welfare*, vol 19, pp 310–20.

Webb, S. (2006) *Social work in a risk society*, Basingstoke: Palgrave Macmillan.

Weick, K. (1987) 'Organizational culture as a source of high reliability', *California Management Review*, vol 29, no 2, pp 112–27.

White, S. (2009a) 'Arguing the case in safeguarding' in K. Broadhurst, C. Grover and J. Jamieson (eds) *Critical perspectives on safeguarding children*, Oxford: Wiley.

White, S. (2009b) 'Fabled uncertainty in social work: A coda to Spafford et al.', *Journal of Social Work*, vol 9, no 2, pp 222–35.

White, S. and Stancombe, J. (2003) *Clinical judgement in the health and welfare professions: Extending the evidence base*, Maidenhead: Open University Press.

White, S. and Wastell, D. (2013) 'A Response to Brown and Ward', www.14gis.co.uk/documents/Response_to_Brown_and_Ward_17th_June.pdf.

White, S., Wastell, D., Broadhurst, K. and Hall, C. (2010) 'When policy o'erleaps itself: the tragic tale of the Integrated Children's System', *Critical Social Policy*, vol 30, pp 405–29.

Wilkinson, I. (2005) *Suffering: A sociological introduction*, Cambridge: Polity.

Wilkinson, R. and Pickett, K. (2009) *The spirit level: Why more equal societies always do better*, London: Penguin.

Williams, B. (1995) *Probation values*, Birmingham: Venture Press.

Williams, F. (2001) 'In and beyond New Labour: Towards a new political ethics of care', *Critical Social Policy*, vol 21, no 4, pp 467–93.

Williams, F. (2004) *Rethinking families*, London: Calouste Gulbenkian Foundation.

Wolf, F. M., Gruppen, L. D. and Billi, J. E. (1985) 'Differential diagnosis and competing hypotheses heuristic: a practical approach to judgement under uncertainty and Bayesian probability', *Journal of American Medical Association*, vol 253, pp 2858–62.

Index

T

U

V

W